Volume 6

THE FOUNDATIONS OF PSYCHOLOGICAL THEORY

THE FOUNDATIONS OF
PSYCHOLOGICAL THEORY

ROBERT E. LANA

Routledge
Taylor & Francis Group

LONDON AND NEW YORK

First published in 1976 by Lawrence Erlbaum Associates, Inc.

This edition first published in 2020
by Routledge
2 Park Square, Milton Park, Abingdon, Oxon OX14 4RN

and by Routledge
52 Vanderbilt Avenue, New York, NY 10017

Routledge is an imprint of the Taylor & Francis Group, an informa business

© 1976 by Lawrence Erlbaum Associates, Inc.

British Library Cataloguing in Publication Data
A catalogue record for this book is available from the British Library

ISBN: 978-0-367-40845-9 (Set)
ISBN: 978-1-00-301614-4 (Set) (ebk)
ISBN: 978-0-367-41811-3 (Volume 6) (hbk)
ISBN: 978-0-367-81632-2 (Volume 6) (ebk)

Publisher's Note
The publisher has gone to great lengths to ensure the quality of this reprint but points out that some imperfections in the original copies may be apparent.

Disclaimer
The publisher has made every effort to trace copyright holders and would welcome correspondence from those they have been unable to trace.

THE FOUNDATIONS
OF PSYCHOLOGICAL THEORY

ROBERT E. LANA

THADDEUS L. BOLTON PROFESSOR OF PSYCHOLOGY
TEMPLE UNIVERSITY

LAWRENCE ERLBAUM ASSOCIATES, PUBLISHERS
1976   Hillsdale, New Jersey

DISTRIBUTED BY THE HALSTED PRESS DIVISION OF

JOHN WILEY & SONS

New York   Toronto   London   Sydney

Lawrence Erlbaum Associates, Inc., Publishers
62 Maria Drive
Hillsdale, New Jersey 07642

Distributed solely by Halsted Press Division
John Wiley & Sons, Inc., New York

Library of Congress Cataloging in Publication Data

Lana, Robert E   1932–
   The foundations of psychological theory.

   Bibliography: p.
   Includes indexes.
   1. Psychology.   2. Psychology—History.
3. Knowledge, Theory of.   I. Title.
BF38.L32   150'.19'09   76-13446
ISBN 0-470-15122-6
               April 9, 1976

Printed in the United States of America

To Jean

Contents

Preface

Over the past decade, like many of my colleagues, I have attempted to understand the enterprise of psychology as a totality. Such an attempt was unpopular in the 1930s, 1940s, and 1950s but has become increasingly more interesting to psychologists today. After some considerable study, I became convinced that the twin vehicles for such a task were the history of the field and the epistemological contexts into which psychological theories fit. The initial chapters of this volume are devoted to explaining, through history, the major epistemological ideas either implicit or explicit in modern psychological theory. Mostly, psychologists do not acknowledge their historical bedfellows. I shall try to put the record straight at least in terms of the ideas developed by various thinkers over the ages, who have directly expounded ways of knowing that are the basis for psychological explanation. It is also true that, in attempting to explain how human beings come to know, one says something about humanity itself. Epistemology must always be both the science of knowing and the science of human beings themselves. Thus, later chapters are studies of the epistemological contexts that, in part, yield modern psychological theory.

Throughout the book, it will be apparent that I have chosen as my dominant theme the constant epistemological interplay between psychological explanation of the human being as object and as subject. The subject–object focus requires a concentrated examination of phenomenology, since few psychologists, with the exception of a handful of clinicians, have had much exposure to it.

The later chapters examine current theoretical forms in personality, social, developmental, and physiological psychology. Clearly, other theoretical areas could have been included, most notably perception and learning. Perception is, however, discussed at some length within the chapters on the history of phenomenology. Learning appears as a problem area within the discussions of behaviorism.

Epistemological considerations, if perceived with sufficient openness, lead eventually to the question of the role of values within psychological theory. I try to deal with this issue in the final chapter.

I would like to thank Ronald Baenninger for leading me to important material relevant to the chapter on physiological theory and Robert Weisberg for aiding me in understanding Chomsky's generative grammar. Clyde Hendrick made helpful suggestions about the entire manuscript.

I would like especially to thank Linda Gattinella, who transcribed tapes and notes, and typed the entire manuscript.

R. E. LANA

THE FOUNDATIONS
OF PSYCHOLOGICAL THEORY

Introduction

Ordinarily it might be thought that the form of explanation is the same regardless of the process to be explained. The nature of explanation is, however, more complicated than it might seem at first glance. There are three major forms of explanation: the predictive, the theoretical, and the phenomenal. The first two are well-known within the context of traditional scientific explanation. The third is somewhat more difficult to deal with, especially if one is used to finding explanations within the framework of science and logic.

PREDICTIVE EXPLANATION

It is possible to observe a given event E follow another event C closely in time. If E invariably or frequently follows C in time, the observer comes to expect that when C occurs E will shortly appear. This expectation is then confirmed by the actual appearance of E. When it is possible for the observer to produce C such that E will occur shortly after, the total observation of C and E is under the control of the observer.

In this case explanation is synonymous with verification by observation. This type of explanation is enhanced by the observer's ability to verify his expectation by manipulating the events rather than by simply observing them passively. We shall see that prediction cannot logically be all there is to say about the constant conjunction of two events. The conjunction gains meaning only when placed within a logico-deductive framework. The combination of this logical framework with consistent empirical observation yields theory.

1

THEORETICAL EXPLANATION

The major characteristic of theoretical explanation is the ability to demonstrate the logically and empirically necessary connections between two or more predictive statements involving the temporal relations between two or more events. That is, a given statement of connection between two or more events must be embedded by logical and empirical ties in a total theoretical structure. Any theory contains explicit or implicit postulates that are statements about the general aspects of the subject matter to be explained. They either are undemonstrated assumptions or are judged to be more or less true based on evidence external to the theory of which they are a part. From these postulates and from a set of definitions of terms, corollaries to the postulates are logically derived. Eventually predictions are derived from the corollaries, and these are tested directly by empirical means. The aspect of the theory in which a particular statement is embedded also enjoys an increment of validity when a successful prediction is made. The more successful the predictions, the more successful the theory. A true theory allows one to derive relationships among variables, which may not have been apparent to the theorist before the construction of the theory. It is clear that theoretical explanation allows for the assimilation of more information than predictive explanation alone.

Both predictive and theoretical explanations are applicable to all sciences for any type of data. Both can yield valid information about the planets, chemicals, kangaroos, or human beings. However, a third form of explanation is possible only when the subject matter of the inquiry is human beings. This is, by far, the most complex and illusive of the three forms of explanation.

PHENOMENOLOGICAL EXPLANATION

To use the terms, "phenomenological" and "explanation" in juxtaposition may actually be a contradiction. However, for the present we shall proceed as if they were not and raise the issue again in a somewhat different context in Chapter 3.

Phenomenological explanation does not fit the conception of experimental science that holds that basic information is gathered by the manipulation of one or more independent variables related to a given dependent variable, all of which are clearly observable. Instead, phenomenology emphasizes direct experience, what it means to the one who experiences, and what he communicates of this experience to others. This process is, of course, a much more difficult task than what the traditional scientist has to communicate, but it offers something beyond the realm of independent–dependent or input–output variables.

When an individual experiences the color red, the love of another person, triumph, triangularity, or orgasm, his direct experience of them is immediately meaningful, and this meaning is separate from *knowledge about* these phenomena. The details of the distinction between phenomena immediately experienced and knowledge of phenomena will be discussed in later chapters. Let it suffice at this point to indicate that fictional literature, art in general, and certain kinds of psychologically oriented descriptions are examples of phenomenal explanation. That is, description of the variety of direct experience possible for human beings is a source of information and insight that is not the same as that provided by predictive or theoretical explanations.

HIERARCHY OF THE SCIENCES

The idea of classifying sciences into a hierarchy in order to understand the relationships among them dates at least to Auguste Comte (Allport, 1968). Although Comte concentrated upon the abstract and practical qualities of the various disciplines of science, I wish to emphasize a different hierarchical aspect, one that should prove more relevant to some of the general themes of this book. The scientific disciplines can be arranged according to the complexity of the unit of study, beginning with those that typically deal with relatively simple phenomena.

If we consider classical, Galilean, mechanical physics, the unit of study is the moving particle. The particle can be the size of an atom, a baseball, or the planet Venus; the principles explaining its movement with regard to its own characteristics (weight, mass, speed) and its relationships to other bodies remain the same. The Newtonian laws indicate this fact. Even though they have been placed within other, more encompassing theoretical systems, and physics has become more complicated in its analyses than the relatively simple Galilean–Newtonian principles would indicate, the motion of particles is still largely the subject matter under study. This is true for field-theoretical physics as well as for the statistical laws of subatomic physics. The subject matter of chemistry derives whatever uniqueness it possesses from the fact that various combinations of molecules form relatively permanent structures (chemicals), which require an analysis different from that provided by physics for the same substances. That is, an analysis of the laws of motion of molecular particles is not sufficient to explain all of their characteristics, especially when they combine. Biology deals with organic matter and the complexity is enormous. The organic matter that forms the living parts of animals and plants is totally subject to the laws of physics and chemistry, but what these disciplines tell us *is not all that can be said about it.* Biology allows us a different set of explanations.

As we proceed up the hierarchy of the disciplines of sciences to physiological psychology, perception, learning, social psychology, sociology, and history, the complexity of the unit being studied increases. Once we reach biology any further delineation yields scientific disciplines that become more and more exclusively concerned with various aspects of human beings. It is as if a human, the scientist, looks outward to objects other than his own body, discovers their properties of motion and combination, applies that knowledge to his own body, then shifts focus and increasingly turns inward to discover other things that are true about himself. This inward turning is an attempt to utilize the assumptions and methods of science to explain various aspects of human existence. The assumption is that the characteristics of human beings are amenable to analysis by the methods of science. We shall see below that this assumption needs to be considerably modified.

Physiological psychology attempts to relate what is biologically true about the organism both to what is behaviorally observable and to what is true about thoughts and emotions that do not have direct behavioral components. Physiological psychology is biology with particular reference to the behavioral components of learning, perception, and emotion, which are correlated with that biology. When one ignores the biological underpinnings of behavior and concentrates only on the behavior itself, then he is dealing with learning, perception, or emotion as they are immediately observable in the organism. Analysis becomes more complex when one concentrates on those determinants of behavior that are social in origin; that is, people or symbols for them, which seem to determine behavior in a manner which is not predictable from other classes of stimuli. Finally, when one is interested not in individual behavior, but in the behavior of a group as a group, then one has reached the realm of sociology and history (to the extent that history may be a predictive enterprise). This entire hierarchy is based upon the assumption that one is interested in predictive and theoretical explanations. The hierarchy's epistemological tenets suggest that a shift to phenomenological explanation may be in order. We shall discuss this issue below. Granting the validity of the hierarchy, a question arises, which is of extreme importance to scientific explanation. Will each of the more complex explanatory levels (corresponding to the increasingly more complex units of analysis) eventually be reduced to the simpler levels of explanation that precede them in the hierarchy? Will it ultimately be possible to reduce all explanations in the hierarchy to the explanations found in physics? In order to answer these questions, it might first be profitable to define "reduction."

Reduction in science may be roughly defined as the process whereby the major principles of the theory to be reduced become some of the minor or derivative principles of another theory. For example, when it was discovered that certain biological activity involving enzymes could be explained within the terms and concepts of chemistry better than within those afforded by theory referring only to biological entities, a reduction was accomplished and the field of biochemistry came into being. A similar type of discovery involving chemical elements and their molecular structure yielded a reduction of certain chemical theory to physical theory. It is important to note, however, that all biological theory has not been reduced to theory in chemistry, nor has all chemical theory been reduced to that of physics. No major reductions have taken place in psychology, since no major theories are sufficiently correct to make such a reduction possible.

Returning to our questions concerning the possibility of reduction within the scientific hierarchy as described above, we can see that either an affirmative or a negative answer to the question would change the way scientists pursue their investigations. For example, if we concentrate on explanation in social psychology, the question becomes whether another person as a stimulus (independent variable) determines behavior in any way essentially different from any nonhuman stimulus or independent variable. If a man tells a woman that he loves her, can we explain his action in terms of reinforcements, sexual or otherwise, that she provides him, and do those reinforcements operate in a manner similar to reinforcements such as food and water, which are known to reinforce nonsocial responses? If this is possible, then explanation regarding the influence of the individual on a social object is reducible to explanation provided within the framework of learning theory, where responses are determined by a variety of reinforcements toward which the human being is biologically attuned, such as food and water. If it is possible to make these reductions in all situations where another individual is a major stimulus, then explanation in social psychology, which utilizes a unique set of concepts, is only of temporary interest, and our efforts should be directed to analyzing social stimuli in terms of their similarities to stimuli invoked in theory in learning and perception. Conversely, if it is not possible to accomplish such a reduction, one interested in social activity ought to focus on its unique aspects.

It is my contention that complete or even major reduction of knowledge about social activity to knowledge existing at other places in the scientific hierarchy is logically impossible. The points of such a position will be dealt with in various chapters concerned with specific subject matter in psychology. It suffices at this point to say that my arguments will focus upon what it means for a human being to acquire and use language and what it means for a human being to think.

1

A Selective History
of Psychological Thought
from the Greeks
to the Early Behaviorists

Pre-Socratic Greek thinkers set the first problem for the Western intellectual, namely, to discover the basic material out of which the universe was formed. The philosophers Leucippus and Democritus offered hypotheses about the nature of the universe that, superficially at least, sound like the atomic theories of today. They believed that the world was composed of small particles, which combined to form various objects, including human beings, in space. This kind of analytic thinking reduced what was to be explained to its component parts and focused early Greek science on the physical or material basis of the universe.

At the time, other philosophers rejected the ultimate validity of the changing physical world and found reality in the permanent nature of ideas, particularly through the use of mathematics. Finally, during the Aristotelian era, there was an attempt to combine the material science of the pre-Socratics with the metaphysics of Plato. Plato and his followers separated the physical from the psychical, that is, body from mind, denegrating the former. This separation permeated Western thought until modern times.

After Plato, the intellectual life of Europe was dominated by attention to man's spiritual and metaphysical nature. For 1500 years, the investigation of man's power to create, develop, and understand ideas was more impressive to Europeans than was an empirical analysis of the world around them. What man was and how he thought took a central place in intellectual life. How objects in the world acted as they did was not as interesting. In short, we may say that the Greeks had developed the two principal Western intellectual proclivities, namely, to look outward and relate human beings and their activities to the activity of objects and to look inward at the nature of self and at the nature of thought.

The Platonic influence on Judeo-Christian thought resulted in the intellectual

7

life of the medieval period being characterized by the idea that man's essential self or spirit was an emanation from a God who was both external to and part of the human being. God was the motive force in man — the final referent. Scholastic philosophy attempted to relate man to God. Because God was seen as ethereal, the most important aspects of man were also ethereal. Hence, man's noncorporeal processes such as thinking, believing, and willing were considered more important than man's bodily processes, which he shared with the lower animals. With the Renaissance in Italy and with the reintroduction of the previously neglected aspects of classical thinking, there began a turning toward the external world once again. This turn laid the framework for the reintroduction of analytic materialistic thinking into Western civilization, such that science took hold in the form in which we know it today. The initial successes of science were in physics and mathematics; the psychology of the day was not yet separable from scholastic theology. The discoveries of Galileo, Kepler, Copernicus, Brahe, and others enabled scientists to predict the movement of earthly and heavenly bodies. By the seventeenth century, mechanical physics was well-established and virtually complete. It was during this century that the first significant modern philosopher emerged. His work contained the two major epistemologies, suggested by the Greeks, that were to become the basis for modern psychology.

DESCARTES (1590–1650)

Both classical Greek and scholastic theories about the nature of human beings placed the primary aspects of existence outside of individuals themselves, although the theories differed as to the nature of these aspects. For Socrates, Plato, and Aristotle, abstract concepts of truth and beauty had an existence separate from the human being, although he was capable of comprehending these ideas and thus elevating his own life. For the scholastic philosophers, an individual gained meaning from his relationship to God. René Descartes changed the shape of Western philosophical thought by the manner in which he turned inward in his inquiries concerning the nature of humanity. His insights allowed successive thinkers to frame questions about the nature of existence in ways that made the human being the center of his own world as Copernicus had discovered the sun to be the center of the physical universe. We may say that psychology begins with Descartes and the questions he framed about human beings. However, there is no sense in which psychology emerges as science and disappears as philosophy. Psychology has always been a product of total thought. This was never more pronounced than in the philosophy of Descartes.

By the seventeenth century it was possible for a philosopher to insist on a logico-mathematical methodology as the means by which one would develop his conceptions of human beings. Descartes discovered the analytical form of geometry and was sufficiently impressed with its power to believe that he could base a theory of humanity upon it. From this beginning it was a simple matter to derive the idea that mathematics is the principal language of understanding, since mathematics could be completed ideationally without reference to either empirical events or concepts such as God. This supposition, common among philosophers of the seventeenth century, led Descartes to depend upon his own processes of rational thought to discover answers to questions concerning the nature of human beings.

Descartes began by eliminating those ideas of which he could not be certain. It was clear to him that any information received through his senses was suspect, since there was abundant evidence to indicate that the senses often deceive us as with hallucinations, illusions, and the ordinary vagaries of daily perception. During sleeping and waking it was possible to have equally vivid impressions of a sensual or emotive kind, but reasoning was more often possible in a waking than a sleeping state. After having eliminated the data of perception and emotion from the area of ontological certainty, Descartes came to a conclusion that was of great significance for Western thought from that point forward. Knowing that the validity of any information could be doubted, Descartes concluded that he could be certain only of the fact of his doubting. He was assured of his own existence by his very thought processes (*cogito ergo sum*). He was confident that reasoning in itself was the method whereby he would come to know, since the act of reasoning rather than information from his senses had brought him to this indisputable knowledge.

This conclusion placed the center of the universe in the human being himself. If the Cartesian *cogito* is true, it would follow that internal subjective processes are the proper study of one who wishes to understand his nature. Actually, whether the *cogito* is true does not disturb the fact that Descartes' influence on later Western thought was enormous, and hence systems derived from his theoretical context must be examined beginning with this subjective premise.

Descartes reasoned as follows: I can imagine that I have no body; that is, I can separate thinking from other processes that "belong" to me, such as the movement of my limbs, the beating of my heart, and so forth. I can also imagine that the world around me does not exist; that is, I could be deceived into thinking it is one thing while it is plainly something else, as one is systematically deceived when he watches the performance of a stage magician. What I cannot imagine is that my thought itself does not exist, because I must be thinking to imagine what is not certain. This also allows me to conclude that whatever else I *believe,* I think. Therefore, I may also conclude that I *am* thought—a conclusion that is similar to that reached by Plato centuries before.

The Platonic position of the centrality of thought in human existence made categories of thought independent of the thinker. The abstract existence of forms of ideas were to be recalled or reconstructed. Plato believed that all men were capable of coming to the same ideas with some effort. Descartes' conclusion stressed the *personal* character of thought rather than its abstract qualities, which existed independent of the thinker. Because an individual thinks anything at all he is certain of his own existence. Coming at a time when science had severely disturbed the centrality of man's position in the universe via the Copernican discoveries and the weakening of the credibility of church dogma as an interpretation of the meaning and scope of life, this conclusion offered seventeenth century man a potential meaning base for his own existence, which he had never really considered before, namely, himself. Bertrand Russell (1945) contended that this was the beginning of modern man's subjective madness, which culminated in various forms of romanticism, some of which are still among us.

In any case, it is clear that Descartes' thinking opened the possibility for a new posture toward the study of the human being's role in the universe. The Platonic Greeks believed in the abstract quality of truth, beauty, and courage, knowledge of which was available to anyone under certain conditions. The scholastic philosophers conceived of human beings in relation to God. Descartes presented the possibility that human beings could examine themselves with their own epistemological processes, since that was all they were certain about in any case.

THE SEPARATION OF MIND AND BODY: THE ROLE OF SCIENCE

Having established that *cogito ergo sum,* Descartes spent a great deal of time in his meditations attempting to demonstrate the existence of God, which need not detain us since we are principally concerned with his epistemology. In the course of his analysis, he came to a conclusion that anticipated the later position of Immanuel Kant regarding understanding: sense data cannot give us all the knowledge that is available to us; understanding, or thought, is necessary to interpret sense data. In this way, he anticipated Kant's categories of mind. His position is simply that there are native proclivities in human beings to classify sense data in a way that is not determined by the sense data. The full impact of this idea will become clear later when we discuss the contribution of Kant. Having established, to his satisfaction, the separation of the understanding from sense data, Descartes concluded that mind and body are separate. His insistence on the separation of mind and body was largely based on his observation that thought processes were clearly different from sensory processes, which were connected to external elements in the environment. His distinction was not a flight of scholastic fancy, but rather set the groundwork for differences that were to continue for the next several hundred years. He was keenly aware that men could create machines that responded superficially the way man himself did. That is, one could build a machine to emit vocables that were very similiar to those emitted by humans, but under no circumstances could the machine be built so as to reply coherently to what was said in its presence. In more modern terms, one could build a machine that was programmed to solve problems, but not a machine that could solve problems with lines of solution that were not already contained within its structure.

Thus Descartes believed that animals and the human body are governed by mechanical principles. These mechanical principles of body interact with the more abstract logico-mathematical principles of mind. He did not question that without body human beings could not function and that the body interacted with the processes of thought. His belief in God led him to the idea that mind or soul was, after death, immortal. However, within life, mind and body are inextricably connected. He considered the nature of the connection and developed a concept of mind – body dualism that has come to be known as interactionism. He speculated that mind – body interaction took place in the central core of the brain, particularly in the pineal gland.

It is clear that if one were to accept Descartes' analysis to this point, there are at least two avenues of study that are possible: one might pursue the nature of the understanding (cognition), that is, one might examine the internal subjective processes of self, or one might pursue the mechanical nature of the body. In a pursuit of knowledge concerning the mechanical nature of the body, one would be bound to compare it with external objects in the environment, since they are also considered to be governed by mechanical processes. In the Western world, these are precisely the two alternatives that were chosen by philosophers and scientists from Descartes' time to the present. One might say that the major Western ideas about human beings can be roughly divided into a pursuit of the subjective or objective character of human beings. Thinkers in non-Western societies have not necessarily reached the bifurcation of Descartes. However, Descartes and those who followed were to become entranced in one way or the other with paths of knowledge that would either turn inward to examine the nature of one's self or turn outward to examine objects in one's environment, with the idea of eventually interpreting the processes of humans themselves in terms of those objects.

LEIBNIZ (1646–1716)

Gottfried Leibniz, like Descartes, believed both in the perfection of God and in mathematics and rationality as the highest forms of human existence. Leibniz's God is rational as are human beings. Since God is rational, He does everything in a most desirable way and the world He created is the best of all possible worlds. This follows from His supreme rationality. All in the world is ordered, nothing is arbitrary; it remains for man to discover the rules by which God has made the world orderly. God and His presumed characteristics were the initial assumptions in Leibniz's thinking as they were for virtually all philosophers to that time. The quality of Leibniz's system may be judged independently of these assumptions, although they are included in our discussion to present a complete idea. His system is perceptual as well as epistemological. With this in mind, the reader need not be detained by the references to God, if they appear outmoded.

Contained in every individual substance or event is the trace of everything that has happened and will happen in the universe. That is, every single substance or object mirrors the entire universe. To explain fully the existence of any single observable or possible energy, one eventually must explain everything in the universe. This position both reflects belief in God's complete sovereignty over existence and anticipates a later philosophical position more in keeping with modern science that knowledge of all events is interactively linked in a logical and empirical manner. To know and understand one object or event requires that one know all those objects and processes that are part of the first and so on until, through an infinite regress, one gains a knowledge of the entire universe of events and objects.

Leibniz, like Descartes, placed thought or cognition in the center of human existence. All of our conceptions do not come from the senses. Thoughts of being, identity, substance, and action, among others, come from an inner subjective experience. That is, human central processes are not able to function independently of the influence upon them of external objects, but bring to the perception of external objects a form that they would otherwise not have. Unlike Descartes, Leibniz did not believe in interaction of body and soul or mind, but rather in a parallelism of the two. His classical analogy was that of two clocks that tell the same time but do not influence one another in any way. Thus, the mechanical aspects of body and the rational aspects of mind, although apparently related, do not influence one another. This separation of mind and body by Leibniz indicated his tacit support of the Cartesian position of separating subjective from objective processes.

MONADOLOGY

For Leibniz, existence was composed of monads; that is, all physical objects and all human processes were thought to be composed of simple substances. Superficially, these substances seem to be atoms similar to those discussed by Leucippus and Democritus in pre-Socratic times. However, the monad is not a structure in the atomic sense, but rather is a process, which can include structures. Monads come together to form composites, which are complex structures. They have neither extension nor form nor divisibility, and they are indestructable. Each monad is different from every other, and any change in a monad comes from its internal principles. They are, therefore, uninfluenced by each other. Because these monads are all a reflection of a central universal monad, which is God, knowing any one of them implies knowing all of them, or the true and complete nature of the universe. The Western God requires a human being with freedom of decision and a central subjective self, which is superordinate to any objective qualities that He may possess.

God apparently has a central position in both the systems of Descartes and Leibniz and is linked with emphasis on subjective processes. However, we have seen with Descartes that, although God still exists in his system, the emphasis has decidedly been placed on the human being as the center of the cognitive universe. Thus we find that although God appears to be central in the system, His role has already been considerably diminished by Descartes' time, and this trend is continued in Leibniz's theories. The active element of the monad is that part given to action that is determined by its own internal principles. The active principle of the substance of existence is perception. Perception itself is a continuous process whereby monads aggregate to form a total entity that forms the process of consciousness (and hence, also, subconsciousness). That is, the processes whereby an unconscious entity becomes conscious are the processes whereby monads, or perceptual entities unconscious in themselves, aggregate to pass the threshold of consciousness.

When perception is accompanied by memory, the resulting substance is called soul (mind). It is clear at this point that Leibniz departed from his analysis of existence into monads with their perceptual qualities and added another ingredient, memory, in order to account for what he considered to be the uniqueness of a human being with a soul (or mind) and, of course, to acount for God Himself, Who must be different from any single monad. The system is weakened by this addition, since memory is present only in human beings and that requires an assumption beyond those related to perception. Nevertheless, Leibniz more specifically than his predecessors, isolated the perceptual process from other processes that could have been placed at the center of the theory of human existence. He also accounted for the gradual shift of ideas from subconsciousness to consciousness in a manner more or less consistent with current interpretations. His system was determined by the properties of God rather than by those inherent in physical objects or human beings. If one discounts the ideas of God, then the deterministic aspects of the system are reduced to the essentially subjective elements that are the unique active principles of human beings. These principles are different from those governing the activity of inanimate objects or animals, or the animal portion of human beings (in the Cartesian sense, such as the mechanics of the body).

Extension (solidity, body) cannot be an attribute of substance if substance is unitary and basic. Therefore, each single substance must be unextended. It also follows that an infinite number of substances (monads) must exist. Each of these has the abstract quality of that of a physical point. From the rejection of extension as an attribute of substance, it follows that each monad is a subjective entity (soul). The only remaining possibility is that the essential attribute of soul is thought. Leibniz thus denied the reality of matter and substituted an infinite number of souls or minds. Since Leibniz, like Descartes, believed that substances cannot interact, there could be no causal relationships among monads. Instead, there is a preestablished harmony — a change in one is mirrored by a change in another.

All systems that include a concept of God also include the idea of a free will in human beings. Leibniz's system was no exception. Even though there is a preestablished harmony in the universe, man is free to make decisions within that preestablished harmony, and these decisions are consistent with the principles of reason. The objectivity of reason and mathematics consists of the total assemblage of points of view of various monads. Subjectivity is the unique perception of each monad, which mirrors the universe from its peculiar perspective. These notions of objectivity – subjectivity suggest an assembly of monads that flow from subjectivity to increasing objectivity. This "flow" is what we now call perception. It is also the process of the rising of consciousness from unconscious elements—the threshold of consciousness being reached when sufficient numbers of elements have arrived at the same point. Since physical objects are also composed of monads, they are similar to thought and other human processes. They also possess a degree of consciousness and, therefore, also a degree of perception. This idea contains Leibniz's sense of the unity of the universe and the similarity between physical and human substances. Because perception and consciousness are the central characteristics of these substances, his universe had a central psychological character, a position in keeping with the *cogito* of Descartes. When this perception is abstractly conceived, Leibniz called it apperception.

Since Leibniz believed that cause is an illusion (monads do not affect one another), perceptual processes are linked with characteristics inherent in the nature of human beings rather than with causal determiners external to the organism. In this sense, he anticipated the later position of Immanuel Kant and later Gestalt psychologists. The notion of preestablished harmony maximizes interest in perception and minimizes interest in causally determined learned phenomena.

Descartes' and Leibniz's principal interests lay in the subjective quality of existence. It was the British who were to focus on an objective evaluation of man, particularly as expressed by the work of John Locke, a contemporary of Leibniz. Thus the philosophical development of man as object awaited the Eighteenth Century and culminated in the work of David Hume.

LOCKE (1632–1704)

Locke's (1690) ideas were essentially continuous with those of Leibniz in that Locke contributed to the development of modern psychological conceptions of human perceptual processes. Locke fully availed himself of the spirit of science as represented by the work of Galileo, Newton, and Harvey. The objective character of perception for Leibniz was contained in the assemblage of monads as they came to rest. This flow of monads was determined by a preestablished harmony. This in turn was determined by God, and man possessed a similar ability to reason and to perceive. Thus, whatever beginning Leibniz made toward characterizing perception and its qualities of consciousness and unconsciousness, he differed from Locke in a major way: Locke essentially removed God from his epistemology. God is an exception to the major ideas of his system.

Locke's concern over the nature of perception directed itself to an analysis of the way the outside world entered the body via the sense organs and the way these sensations, in turn, were handled as ideas. With Locke, physical science provided the basis for the method and the direction of inquiry about human beings. The juxtaposition of Leibniz and Locke indicates how a later separation of the idea of sensation from the idea of perception occurred. The actual process of an object or event entering the body via the sense organs and what that entailed constituted sensation. The eventual message to the brain and how it was handled there constituted the study of perception. Most psychologists no longer make this distinction. However, the distinction, as it emerged in the Nineteenth Century, was set by the kind of thinking that produced the inward-turning subjective interpretation of perception of Leibniz and the object-related interpretation of Locke.

In Locke's time, the concern among philosophers, particularly the British, was to determine the content and process of mind, this through an analysis of perception. Locke was convinced that the appropriate study for man was man himself and particularly his central processes such as thinking and perceiving. The analytic spirit of science allowed Locke to think of the mind as composed of elements or units, which were ideas. Thus, an idea was the object of thinking, and the mind was analyzable into ideas. Locke became interested in the content of the mind rather than how people come to hold the ideas that they do. Consequently, a question arose as to how ideas become connected to one another to form the ebb and flow of thought. The association of ideas, an Aristotelian notion, had already been discussed in detail by Locke's predecessor Thomas Hobbes. This concept became the principle whereby ideas were connected.

Ideas are generated from two sources, sensation and reflection. In holding the notion that an idea can come from a sensory experience, Locke remained consistent with Leibniz. However, the development of a sequence of ideas from sensation was a somewhat different idea than the Liebnizian notion of a prearranged harmony of sensations and ideas. For Locke, it was clear that an idea *comes from* experience. Objects in the outside world are transmitted to the content of mind. Since this involves the various organs of perception such as the ears, nose, and eyes, an intrinsic linkage was established between the generation of an idea and the functions of various parts of the body.

Locke also believed that it was possible to have an idea about something without actually having to perceive it in the first place. Locke understood that certain concepts, such as those of mathematics, were not necessarily perceptual in origin. The mind knows its own process by reflection. This appears in nature only in man and God.

Ideas are either simple or complex. Simple ideas are unanalyzable, but complex ideas can be analyzed into simple ideas. Simple ideas are combined in a manner analogous to chemical combinations to form complex ideas. The principles of association, which we will discuss below, are the rules by which the combination of simple ideas occurs.

PRIMARY AND SECONDARY QUALITIES OF IDEAS

Locke subdivided simple ideas into their primary and secondary qualities. Primary qualities are those that inhere in bodies and are singularly perceived by the senses: for example, solidity, motion, and number. Secondary qualities are characteristics that objects possess that produce ideas that do not exist in the form in which they are perceived: for example, colors, sounds, and tastes. The later Nineteenth Century distinction between sensation and perception is based ostensibly on Locke's separation of ideas into primary and secondary qualities. It can be seen by the modern reader that the distinction is more apparent than real. Later perception psychologists have obliterated the distinction between primary and secondary qualities and between sensation and perception. In short, there seems to be no empirical or logical grounds for separating primary and secondary qualities: for example, the idea of number (a primary quality) from color (a secondary quality). For Locke, these qualities resided in the nature of the object, whereas for Leibniz they were an extension of a general perceptive process that ultimately emanates from God and resides, by derivation, in the subjective process of human beings. Thus, for Locke, the characteristics of objects themselves directly determined the way a human organism thinks about them. This notion instituted the concept that human thought has an objective character. With the introduction of the notion of secondary qualities, Locke could complete his analysis of the nature of thought. That is, although it may be clear that light emanating from a red object must strike the eye of the viewer in order for him to *see* red, it is not clear how this redness becomes part of the thought process of the organism on the basis of that physical fact alone; hence, the notion of a secondary quality that requires an interaction of the physiological with the perceptual–cognitive character of the subject in order ultimately to produce the idea of redness.

Since observation of the nature of objects as they enter perception was so central to Locke's thinking, he may be regarded as the founder of empiricism —the notion that all knowledge is derived from experience. He excepted logic and mathematics, God and a sense of self. These exceptions were to prove extremely important for later developments in epistemology. Although Locke was still not ready to eliminate concepts of God, self, and mathematics from his epistemology, his did represent a bold innovation from the ideas of Descartes and Leibniz, both of whom depended heavily on the subjective character of ideas. For Locke, there was no separation of man from not man since most ideas are derivable from the nature of objects themselves. There is thus a fusion of the physical world and human beings to form a particular epistemological position, that of empiricism. He also believed that we experience sensations, but not their causes, thus allowing for the later subjective idealism of Berkeley. Locke assumed that our sensations are caused and that these causes resemble, to some extent, the sensations that they cause. However, as we shall see later, the belief that sensations have causes must be made on other than empirical grounds.

DAVID HUME (1711-1776)

Although it can be argued that David Hume (1961) was not the most important or insightful of the Eighteenth Century British empiricists, it is clear that his thinking represents the culmination of that tradition. He explicitly stated that all sciences and all intellectual endeavors including those of mathematics and philosophy begin with the science of understanding human beings. This position is a culmination of work begun by Descartes and continued by Leibniz and Locke, which placed epistemology in the center of intellectual activity. By implication, psychology is part of this nucleus.

Like Locke, Hume was an empiricist and assumed that all knowledge stems from experience. For Hume, the initial human experience was the impression that is simply a sensation. From these impressions arise simple ideas, which exactly represent, and which are always preceded by, their corresponding impressions. With this fundamental notion Hume became involved in the idea of cause and effect and in the making of inferences. The combination of simple ideas forming complex ideas was explained in a manner similar to Locke, as we have discussed above. Every simple idea has a corresponding simple impression, although complex ideas do not necessarily have corresponding complex impressions. Since impressions and ideas are in constant conjunction with one another, impressions are formed both by objects in the world and from reflections, so that the basic unit of perception is also producible by thought.

Ideas are combined and connected through the process of association, which is brought about by resemblance, contiguity, and cause and effect:

Resemblance. Because of similar elements existing in ideas, the presence of one idea introduces or recalls another.

Contiguity. When two ideas are always together in space and time the presence of one calls up the other idea.

Cause and Effect. The combination of cause and effect occurs when the presence of one idea (or an event in space–time) seems to compel or produce necessarily another idea (or event).

This is the most forceful of the three conditions of association. It is also a notion that was difficult to comprehend for Hume. Since the power by which one idea produces another idea cannot be discovered by examination of either one or both of the ideas involved, it follows that cause and effect are relations of which we receive information from experience and not from abstract reasoning. This position depends on the fact of experience to the exclusion of an abstract initial assumption to explain the process of cause and effect. Here we see an intensified centering upon experience as the producer of a force heretofore thought of as an abstract idea, a concept that was not present in Descartes or Leibniz and only partially developed in Locke.

Hume made the final jump of defining an abstract idea such as cause and effect in terms of immediate experience rather than in terms of an abstract entity. When two objects are presented to the senses and there are certain relations of one to another (for example, one object appears behind another object) this is perception and has nothing to do with reason. It is directly given. Where the mind need not go beyond perception to understand the relationship existing between objects, the experience of cause and effect allows the human understanding to go beyond immediately given perception and produces the idea of necessary connection between two objects. From it, we are at least assured that the existence of one object was perceived or followed by the existence of another object.

If we observe the constant conjunction of two objects or their constant remoteness from one another, there is nothing in the objects themselves that allows us to conclude that they are always in this relationship. We do conclude that there is some as yet undiscernible cause that unites or separates them. Thus, of the three major relations involved in the association of ideas (resemblance, contiguity, and cause and effect) only cause and effect may involve processes beyond our senses. Since cause and effect associated with the two objects is a simple idea, it followed for Hume that it must have an accompanying impression. Clearly, such an impression cannot be found in any quality of the two events involved in cause and effect since they are simple objects or events, which can be found in noncausal relations. Also, a third object or event may have qualities completely unlike the first two, but may fall into a cause and effect sequence with them. The idea of causation, therefore, must be derived from some relation among objects.

Hume discovered that objects need to be contiguous in space and time in order to be perceived as existing in a causal relationship to one another. As we have noted, the principle of contiguity is also a characteristic of association, without necessarily implying causality. The issue becomes somewhat clouded at this point. Apparently, simple ideas can be associated by means of contiguity in space and time without the idea of cause and effect emerging. However, the principal basis of a complex idea of cause and effect is that of contiguity in space and time. They are not contradictory ideas, but the issue is further muddied if we consider that Hume conceived that all objects or events can be either cause or effect. The consistency of Hume's position can be shown by the following statements:

1. All objects can be cause or effect.
2. Any two given objects in contiguity with one another in space or time often produce simple ideas of association, but not necessarily ideas that involve the idea of cause and effect.
3. Two objects perceived in a cause and effect relation to one another are always contiguous in space or time.

Besides the relation of contiguity, a second relation is that of priority in time of the cause to the effect.

At this point in his thinking, Hume made the remarkable conclusion that he could discover no other relations that are relevant to the idea of causation. Thus, the classical notion of a cause *compelling* or *necessitating* an effect was temporarily rejected by Hume, since he could discover only contiguity and order in the cause and effect relationship. He denied the logical legitimacy of the classical concept of necessary connection in cause and effect, but did assert that we have an *idea* of necessary connection between the cause and effect, since all objects in this relationship indicate contiguity and priority in time of one with the other. It therefore followed for Hume that every event that has a beginning does not necessarily have a cause. He argued that we can imagine a nonexisting event for the first time without the principle of necessity being conjoined with this process. It therefore can be assumed with equal facility that an event occurs with a cause or that it occurs without a cause. Since the idea of necessity is neither derived from logical reasoning nor directly observable, the question arises of how individuals experience an idea of causation. Apparently some type of individual experience forces upon a person the notion of the necessity of an effect following its cause.

Although surprised by his discovery that the essential ingredient of the idea of cause and effect was that of constant conjunction, Hume felt small satisfaction with this solution and believed that it advanced understanding of causation but little. Hume realized, as anyone would, that he felt compelled to believe that necessity was part of cause and effect. His temporary conclusion that constant conjunction seemed the only objective element associated with causation was unsatisfactory. Necessity seemed to be a common sense portion of the concept of causation, yet he could not legitimately introduce it as a distinct meaningful idea in his analysis. He thought that a solution might be forthcoming in the idea of the repetition of the events that were believed to be in a causal relationship. That is, he conceived that necessary connection might be

inferred in the circumstance or repeated observations of the constant conjunction of events. Even this he felt to be an uncomfortable solution. Today we
know it to be no solution at all.

In retrospect, we are not surprised at Hume's dilemma. Given the firmly
entrenched empiricism of his day with the accompanying emphasis on sense
data as the origin of any epistemological consideration, his conclusion was
foregone. With some exceptions, he believed the process of thought to have
characteristics that were the same as those of the objects of sense. If ideas
could not be accompanied by an appropriate object impression the idea itself
(for example, that of cause and effect) was deemed to be false. Having
established the position that man's understanding could be analyzed in the same
way as the objects of understanding, one may easily fall into the trap of
believing that there cannot be ideas that are independent of the nature of
objects. Hume provided the *reductio ad absurdum* for Locke's empirical
beginning. However, Hume's *reductio* did provide new ideas about the nature
of thinking in general and about inferences and cause and effect in particular.
Often one finds that any important idea is eventually driven to its *reductio ad
absurdum,* and those who accomplish this provide the service, sometimes
inadvertedly, of measuring the limitations of an idea.

Immanuel Kant was intrigued with Hume's dilemma and continued to explore
the relationship of ideas to objects. Kant's proposed solution to the problem
was already contained as the germ of an idea in the following of Hume's
observations: In discussing the relation between cause and effect and necessary
connection, his argument yielded one conclusion that was of historical significance. Since any idea either arises from an impression or is a combination of
simple ideas, the idea of necessity must either arise from some impression or be
a combination of simple ideas. Hume demonstrated that there is no impression
that can give rise to a legitimate idea of necessity in the external world. He also
could not imagine what simple ideas combined to form the complex idea of
necessity, which seemed so basic to him. The only possible explanation
remaining for Hume was that the psychological propensity in the individual that
allows him to pass from the impression of an object to the idea of the object is
the condition that allows the idea of necessity. The implication here is that the
idea of necessity may be part of the native understanding that an individual
brings to a cause and effect situation. It is in this sense that Hume anticipated
Kant. Besides the rather central idea of cause and effect, Hume was concerned
with the nature of other ideas that he also saw as basic to the understanding,
such as the ideas of substance, unity, abstraction, and extension.

Substance, Unity, and Abstract Ideas.   The idea of substance is a
collection of simple ideas that are united by imagination and have a particular
name assigned to them. Abstract ideas such as quality or quantity are no
different from a quality or quantity itself. One cannot separate the actual length

of a line from the line itself. Thus Hume concluded that it is impossible to separate the conception of a thing as an abstract idea from the idea of a particular. Abstraction for Hume became simply a question of resemblance among specifics and a tendency to give a name to this resemblance.

Extension.   The idea of extension is given by the object, which is part of the impression formed from it. For example, viewing a table is sufficient to give rise to the idea of extension. There is a problem with this concept. It is possible for the idea of extension to exist independently of any particular perception an individual may have. That is, it may remain an abstract concept. Although it may be true that experiences involving sense perceptions are necessary for the idea of extension, they cannot account for the idea itself since, by Hume's own admission, only specific physical characteristics are conveyed by the data of the senses. Therefore, the idea of extension would have had to arise from this particular experience and not be one-to-one with it. It is clear that the dificulty here is the same difficulty that Hume recognized in his analysis of cause and effect. There is a tendency for people to infer causality in a compelling sense. There is a tendency for people to abstract ideas like extension (and also substance and unity). Yet it is also clear that these abstractions cannot be a direct result of the characteristics of the objects themselves. If abstractions are not contained in the characteristics of perception or sense data or in the characteristics of objects themselves, the only remaining explanation is that they are part of what it means to think as a human being.

Space and Time.   Hume understood that he must deal with certain classical problems in order to test the reliability of his system. Philosophers have always dealt with ideas such as space, time, points, and surfaces. In order to be consistent, it was necessary for Hume to trace these concepts to their sense impression origins or to deal with them in some unique way. For Hume, the ideas of space and time were not separate and distinct, but merely concerned the relative order in which objects exist. He did not realize that the ideas of order and relationship are in themselves distinct ideas separate from the objects to which they relate. Points and surfaces also do not admit to further divisibility. Equality is interpreted similarly. It is sufficient to present two objects that are equal in order to give us a notion of this concept. The notion of equality and inequality is derived from the whole appearance and the comparison of a particular group of objects. There are three propositions that are distinguishable; greater than, less than, and equal to. These explanations suffer the same difficulty as those applied to space and time, extension, substance, and unity. They are not derivable from the same terms Hume used to express what people see and hear, such as tables or chairs. He insisted on a kind of operationalism when he maintained that a notion of correctness of perception of equality beyond what we have instruments or techniques to make is useless as well as incomprehensible. The standard of perfection of equality is formed by making repeated corrections and in comparing these with some rule of which we have some assurance by virtue of repeated examination trials. It is from these corrections and by carrying out the same action of mind, even when its reason fails us, that we form the loose idea of the perfect standard without being able to understand or comprehend it. Again, what Hume missed was the fact of the operation of the mind separately from the objects it perceives. In short, if space and time and equality are relational in nature, they cannot be totally given by the nature of the objects themselves.

Existence.   Since we never remember any idea or impression without attributing existence to it, the idea of existence must either be derived from a distinct impression or must be the same idea as the perception or object. It is clear that the idea of existence is not derived from any particular impression. Hume concluded that the idea of existence is the same as the idea of what we conceive to be existence. There is no need to point out for this instance, the continuing difficulty that Hume had in dealing with abstract concepts because of his wedding to sense data.

The Humean Dilemma.   The problem permeating all of Hume's discussion of the various entities of cognition lies in the conflict between his empiricism and its success in dealing with sense data and its failure in dealing with thought. He noticed that human beings apparently have knowledge only of what they can see, feel, hear, and touch. However, he was also stymied in that he could not demonstrate through the senses the character of thought, for example, the inference of an a effect from a cause. His difficulty arose because sensation and perception are described mainly in terms of the physics of the object or the biology of peripheral mechanisms such as the eye or the ear. He was less concerned with the operation of the brain as manifested in thought.

It was for later theorists to recognize that the organism is active and contributes as much to an understanding of objects as they contribute understanding to it. It might be said that the fallacy of Hume's objectivism is that thought processes were forced into categories that were derived from the nature of physical objects and should have been derived from their own intrinsic characteristics. Hume and the British empiricists had taken the definite step of equating human thought processes with object processes. Hence, they saw most of the workings of human beings as objectlike. The legacy of classic scholastic and Greek thought that placed human thinking in the center of the universe was lost even though their emphasis on mind as central to human processes was overdone and had obscured the possibilities for empirical observation and therefore for characterizing human beings in part, as understandable in terms similar to those used in explain objects.

However, in no way should the contribution of Hume, Locke, and the British empiricists be minimized, although they were in a kind of error and this error was to persist into the twentieth century. They provided an epistemological basis that allowed the growing science of the day to continue and, indeed, to further concentrate on dealing with the world and man as objects. This was necessary if science was to blossom and to be extended into an examination of all the processes of human beings. History has almost always shown that an idea that is worthwhile is eventually carried to its *reductio ad absurdum* by disciples of those who introduce it. This is necessary to develop the full usage of the concept or theory and to bring it its highest fruition. It has remained for later generations to recognize limits and to turn in other corrective directions. By the late eighteenth century the thesis and antithesis of subject and object were posed, and it was possible to clearly recognize them as the two great possibilities in Western thought. They were linked with the philosophies of Plato and Aristotle as well as those succeeding them and with the new science of the day, which had not as yet reached its peak, but was to show a tremendous surge in the nineteenth century. When Hume's work was complete, the older subjectivism of the scholastics was not fit to provide an antithesis. It remained for Kant to perform this task.

CAUSALITY AS A SUBJECTIVE QUALITY: IMMANUEL KANT (1724–1804)

Kant (1961) was challenged by Hume's dilemma. He saw Hume's work as raising one of the most fundamentally important questions in philosophy — to what extent does an understanding of objects in space differ from an understanding of the nature of man? Hume could not find necessity in cause and effect in the objects that entered into that relationship, nor in any principle of logic. Kant directed his attention to the one remaining locus where necessity might lie.

By the later eighteenth century, direct sense experience was accepted by virtually all thinkers as inextricably linked to the process of understanding. Kant accepted this proposition. The question for him became, how does sense experience become transformed into knowledge? It had to come from the relationship between what human beings are and what they experience. It will be remembered that the British empiricists, including Hume, could not handle apparently valid ideas such as self and mathematics (God was also an idea excluded from knowledge of sense data, but because of special problems associated with it, we shall not discuss it within this epistemological context). Thus, the challenge was to account for the origins of mathematics, logic, and, indeed, any abstract idea that was not simply a label for a collection of impressions via sense experience. Kant argued that although none of our knowledge can transcend experience, it is nevertheless in part a priori and not inferred inductively from experience. Mathematics and logic are a priori. An empirical proposition is one that we can know through sense perception. An a priori proposition is one that, although it may be elicited by experience, is seen to have a basis other than experience. Causality is known a priori. This was Kant's solution to Hume's dilemma. One may say then that necessity is a way that a human being has of dealing with certain of his experiences and that this way is independent of any particular experience.

Causality is necessarily presupposed in the knowing of an ordered experience. Kant distinguished between knowing the merely subjective order of our apprehension and knowing the objective following of events. He gave two examples: If we apprehend a house by successively apprehending the different parts of it, there is no necessity at beginning at the roof and then going to the basement. We can start at the basement and then work our way up to the roof, just as easily. We do not regard either of these sets of successive perceptions as representing anything characteristic of the house. On the other hand, if we see a ship moving down a river our apprehension of its place higher up in the course of the river must come first. It is impossible in the apprehension of this phenomenon that the ship should be perceived first below and then higher up. Here the order in the succession of our apprehensions is determined and our apprehension regulated by that order. We are compelled to apprehend the ship as going down stream. We cannot reverse at will the order and apprehend the ship as going up stream as we can reverse at will the starting point of our perception of the house. In order to distinguish objective succession from subjective succession we must regard the former as compelling to our perception; that is, in order to be apprehended as objective, succession must be understood as necessitated by causal connections. The category of causality is a logical presupposition made by the individual of the objective succession of events in time. All objective knowledge of phenomena with regard to their relationship in the succession of time depends on the category of causality.

Unlike Hume who could find only psychological, that is, nonrational qualities in the idea of cause and effect, Kant attempted an epistemological argument for the validity of the *idea* of cause and effect. Kant's idea of objective apprehension began with the notion that experience translates into perception only through epistemological considerations, which are given in the basic nature of the organism.

The outer world causes only the nature of sensation. Our mental apparatus orders this matter in space and time and supplies the concepts by means of which we understand experience. Space and time are subjective in that they are part of our apparatus of perception. There are other a priori categories besides causality and space and time, but it is unimportant to enumerate them here.

Although for many there are difficulties with Kant's ideas, the form of his solution to the cause and effect and similar problems should not be difficult for the modern reader to appreciate. We do not find strange the fact that elephants cannot fly, and one of the best explanations for this fact is that the structure of their body simply does not allow it. We are not surprised that our arms can bend in only one direction once we have examined the nature of the socket around the elbow. The point is that the growth of structure over evolutionary time quite often determines or limits function. Why is it not also possible that through the same evolutionary time the human brain and central nervous system came to develop to the point where certain functions in the form of "categories of mind" or ways of perceiving objects have developed much the same as the gross anatomy of elephants has developed and is related to their behavior?

With the work of Kant the two great directions that psychology was to take in the Nineteenth and Twentieth Centuries were epistemologically set. It should be clear to the reader that the differences between Hume and Kant may only be differences in chronology. Had Hume lived as long as Kant, they might have come to much more agreement than is apparent in their major works. Kant was an extension of Hume. Hume saw the problem and Kant made a dialectical attempt at solution. Through the Nineteenth and Twentieth Centuries, we shall see that the ideas of the two men were treated as somehow in opposition. This was not true in terms of the evolution of the problem. Despite this, there is a certain legitimacy to separating subjectivism from objectivism in a variety of ways within the framework of psychology.

THE NINETEENTH AND TWENTIETH CENTURIES

By the nineteenth century the physical and biological sciences had become thoroughly empirical. By and large they followed the epistemological lead of the British empiricists. Since the terms of human understanding did not enter physical or biological theory, questions of subject and object did not arise. However, the problems that did arise for scientists and philosophers concerned with explaining the nature of human existence were considerably different. The Humean idea that the contingency of events was the only legitimate element discoverable in an empirical relationship allowed nineteenth century empiricists to carry forward scientific research on a sure footing. There is not a more conservative and superficially sound epistemological position than the one that depends principally upon the functional contingency of events as the ingredients of explanation. By not being concerned with the idea of necessity, or any more complex notion, wild speculation and other excesses could be removed from the inferential process. Although this position was not necessarily Hume's, it was the position that was formed out of the Humean concerns by nineteenth century thinkers, and it carried into the twentieth century. The Kantian response to Hume became essentially lost to science during most of the nineteenth century perhaps because the scientific examination of sense data was more consistent with the Humean emphasis. Thus, by the end of the nineteenth century, an epistemology developed, which came to view human beings as objectlike in this functional-contingency sense. In short, if sense data can be examined best by input–output functional concepts and techniques, and if sense data is the basis of human existence, it could be (and was) argued that all or most human responses can be examined by these same techniques and concepts. The fallacy of this argument has already been discussed.

Although there were periods of intellectual quiessence, the reiteration of the subject–object theme is so persistent it extends into the twentieth century. We shall see that ultramodern theories of psychology reflect the dialectic's oppositional nature. The superimposition of the science of the seventeenth and eighteenth centuries upon the scholasticism of previous centuries required a wrenching apart of these two sensibilities, one of which was to focus upon man as subject and the other upon man as object. The focus upon man as object allowed an accumulative sort of success. The task was easier. It was simpler to analyze the properties of human beings as objects than to examine them as the source of their own cognitive processes. It was possible for a science of human beings to build a clear, relatively flexible methodology, which could be applied to problems of physiology, perception, and learning. The great success of science was in its power to predict and control, and to the extent that a science of psychology succeeded, it was along similar dimensions. Dealing with a human being as subject was a more complicated task, one that remained somewhat estranged from the growing scientific enterprise.

The nineteenth century thinker who was sympathetic to Hume's position had a clear mandate to proceed in a certain fashion to understand the nature of man. If simple ideas are derived from impressions that, in turn, are exact copies of objects, then it is clear that the primary problem in understanding human beings is to understand the relationship between objects in space and impressions and ideas about them. The Humean emphasis determined, in part, the epistemological principles by which nineteenth century psychological science was to develop along one of two bifurcated paths. The problem became narrowed to a question of how an object in space was taken in as a bit of information by a human being and how he reacted to it. The specific nineteenth century experimental problems thus asked such initial questions as how man comes to see, hear, smell, and taste. Sensation and perception became the first problems for experimental psychology. Interestingly, those scientists who were sensitive to the Kantian arguments regarding the nature of thought also believed that perception posed the first problems for a science of psychology. This belief followed from Kant's assumption that experience is the initial stage of knowledge. Thus the initial aspect of experience is the transmittal of objects in the world to the sensorium of the human being. Hence, for Kant's followers objects in space were given part of their meaning by the fact that they were apprehended by human beings with certain distinct native characteristics of perceiving and thinking.

THE PHILOSOPHY OF SCIENCE
IN THE LATE NINETEENTH AND
EARLY TWENTIETH CENTURIES

In the late nineteenth century, Ernst Mach (1959) formalized the objective stance in the study of psychology. In so doing, he became one of the first formal epistemologists of science. Mach's contribution to an understanding of the nature of psychological analysis was his interpretation of the nature of physical, biological, and psychological data. The data of all science is perceptual. The physicist and biologist record their perceptual processes in analyzing movement in inorganic bodies, plants, and animals. Thus, perceptual processes, which are epistemologically the first subject matter of psychology, are seen as the basic data of all sciences. This is a more precise interpretation of the older idea of the unity of thought and knowledge; that is, the unity of science. Thus, the bases of all science are the colors, sounds, odors, and so forth, that are available to all human beings. The arrangements of these colors, sounds, and odors and their relations to a functioning human organism form the basic explanatory system of science whether of a perceptual or physical nature. Clearly, this basis is ultimately more important for a science of psychology than it is for a science of physics since, by definition, psychology maintains a focus on this initial perception, whereas physics infers beyond it to the physical world.

Mach noted that because of the extensive development of mechanical physics a kind of higher reality is ascribed to the spatial and temporal. The temporal and spatial links among colors, sounds, and odors seem more real than the colors, sounds, and odors themselves. In this scheme, space and time might just as appropriately be called sensations as colors, sounds, and odors. The senses neither represent things rightly or wrongly nor are they always reflective of the dimensions and attributes of a physical object. Hence, the reality of the senses or sense data is as compelling as physical reality. Sensation is as real as are the facts of physics. Although the reality of sensations in themselves is assured, Mach believed that ego concepts, which were abundant in the late nineteenth century, gave rise to pseudoproblems. He believed that there are physical bodies, stimuli, bodily characteristics, and central nervous system processes such as volitions and memory images. It is the volitions and memory images that compose what people label the ego. Hence, ego concepts are merely summary devices for certain parts of human existence. To conceive that a term such as ego refers to an emergent or separate process is to fall into a solipsistic trap. Hence, there cannot be an antithesis between physical stimuli and ego, or between ego and physiological stimuli. There is no antithesis between ego and world. A gulf appears between physical and psychological research only when we acquiesce to our habitual separation of self from the rest of the world.

Mach attempted to eliminate the mind–body dichotomy. His argument was similar to Hume's; namely, that mind and body are convenient ideas for use in practical affairs, but eventually take on a reality that they do not actually possess since they represent a false dichotomy in the first place. We have seen that Hume dealt with the cause and effect problem in a similar fashion. The ego, therefore, must be given up as a viable concept. In science nothing is important except that it can be observed or is logically sound, and everything hypothetical or metaphysical is superflous and should be eliminated. If we are to consider the ego as a real entity, we become involved in the following dilemma: Either we juxtapose the ego with a world of unknowable entities (the Berkeleyan problem) or we must regard the world including the egos of other people as structured in our own ego (solipsism). Colors, sounds, spaces, and times are the elements whose given connections we must investigate. For example, Marriotte discovered that a certain spot on the retina is blind. The physicist was accustomed to identifying a point on the retinal image with every spatial point and a sensation with every retinal point. Yet we know that the blind spot gap is filled out in normal vision. The problem is created by asking the question in physical terms. When this question is eliminated from psychological inquiry, no problem exists at all. A defect of light sensation cannot be noticed at a spot blind from the beginning.

For Mach, concepts like "will" had to be explained by means of the physical forces of the organism alone. The first developed reflexes in young animals are the beginnings of the dominant reflex system that becomes sinew reflexes in adults. Hence, "will" becomes nothing more than a learned conditioned reflex. Thus, Mach anticipated the conditioning demonstrations of Pavlov and Thorndike at the turn of the twentieth century. The characteristic aspect of voluntary action as distinct from reflex movement lies in the subject's recognition that the dominating factor in the voluntary action is his own representation that anticipates it. He recognizes that sensations alone cannot constitute a psychic mental life. Will also requires that association and memory be possible. Memory involves physical traces in the central nervous system. Every chemical process in the organism leaves traces that increase the probability of the same process. Mach believed that there was little in the physical world that was analogous to the process of memory.

This was before the development of complex computers. Mach noted that the fundamental feature of psychic life was that of two contents of consciousness, which originally have appeared together. The reoccurrence of one tends to produce the appearance of the other. He did not propose, however, to reduce all elements of psychic life to this mechanism. He assumed that spontaneous psychological processes not due to association probably existed and excited neighboring parts of the nervous system.

Mach tempered his stance by concluding that, although ultimately all explanations of phenomena may be made by referring to physical dimensions, no one at the time (1896) had developed such a system. Therefore, more successful explanations of various apparent nonphysical phenomena can be made along different dimensions; for example, the biologist is more successful than the physicist in explaining life process.

Mach recognized that human beings act as if they have egos. That is, an individual believes he has a center or self, which is the core of his own existence and which presumably controls the way he sees and deals with his life. Hume, although failing to discover its logical or empirical basis, also saw that people assumed that there was such a thing as productive cause. Both Mach and Hume concluded that this was an error in thinking. Hume was uncomfortable with this conclusion. Mach was not. Although he removed an ancient prejudice retarding the scientific study of man, he replaced it with a subtle one of his own: the necessary reduction of complex concepts to simple ones. In any case, there is no doubt that Mach cleared away many useless methodologies and concepts in psychology. Besides striking a blow for the objective empirical movement of the nineteenth century, his conclusion that the fundamental data of science for both physicists and psychologists is sensation strongly influenced later thought, especially the Gestalt position. Gestalt psychology, which assumes the fundamental unity of scientific explanation, also makes sensation the central data of its investigations. Mach's position that colors, sounds, and odors are products of the interaction of physical objects and the reacting organism, allowed him to emphasize the need to examine the total configuration presented by object and perceiver. His position also contributed to the Gestalt formulation of isomorphism between behavioral (in the Gestalt sense) and physiological processes. Mach called this concept "the principle of the complete parallelism of the psychical and physical [p. 60]." It is clear that Mach's concern with objectivity did not exclude the kinds of problems that Immanuel Kant dealt with as well. The subjective quality of human beings about which Kant wrote was contained as a concept in Mach's relational ideas concerning sensation and perceiver. Consequently, although Mach gave great impetus to the objectivity of the twentieth century, particularly behaviorism, he was not without contribution to the subjectivism that was to lead to twentieth century phenomenology.

EVOLUTION

In the middle of the nineteenth century, a body of data was collected which supported a position that eventually gave great impetus to developing objective psychology. Charles Darwin's *The Origin of Species* appeared in 1859 and was based upon his collection of a mass of data supporting a concept of evolution. The idea had been conceived before Darwin, but the evidence he amassed yielding certain modification of earlier ideas was very convincing. The notion was that there was a natural selection of animals and plants, in that, by chance, variations of inheritable characteristics allowed certain organisms to survive their environment. They transmitted these characteristics genetically to their offspring, and the species they represented developed in those directions. Since environmental changes were not always great, a number of organisms within any one species tended to remain relatively stable over long periods of time. Since food supplies were generally limited, organism and environment were in a state of balance.

Darwin believed that, accompanying this process of survival of the fittest, there was a tendency for one species to evolve into different forms over eons of time. This implied that the evolution of a single species might produce, over a long period of time, an almost totally different organism. However, the differences among the organisms were not so great that similarities were not evident. Besides intraspecific similarities, there are also interspecific similarities. For example, insects and men have similar structures if you consider they both have legs, eyes, and abdomens. It is also evident that these structures are involved in similar functions such as walking, seeing, and eating. Since many species, however divergent in structure, often live in close proximity, it is not surprising that they have developed similar ways of dealing with their environment. Hence, among mammals, the structure and function of the viscera of a rat and gorilla might be remarkably similar although the external features of both animals are very different. These similarities presumably allow similar conclusions to be reached about the precise functions of various organs.

The evidence for Darwin's position, although remaining in part controversial, was overwhelmingly impressive to the scientists of the day and greatly influenced biological and psychological sciences. In psychology, as well as biology, the idea took hold that it was now possible to study infrahuman organisms in order to gain information about human beings. Darwin, as well as others, believed that there was continuity in both function and structure between animals and humans. Biologists and psychologists made the choice of studying various infrahuman species in order to gain more control over a subject's environment, a condition limited in human research by ethical considerations.

With the idea of animal and human continuity through evolution, there was a tendency on the part of scientists to emphasize behavioral similarity between animals and humans and to bracket concepts such as consciousness or mind. They emphasized sensory and behavioral output in animal studies because these were accessible and easily generalizable to human beings. This tendency further strengthened the theory of evolution. Indeed, animals could not communicate in a manner that scientists could easily label conscious because they could not communicate via language. The lack of language allowed some scientists of the late nineteenth and twentieth centuries to conclude that behavior was the most important aspect of *human* activity rather than consciousness or mind. The theory of evolution lent support to a great deal of information gathering and theory building with respect to biological and behavioral characteristics of both animals and human beings. Since it was now plausible that there was no break in continuity, the similarities of the two were emphasized, and hence "consciousness" and "mind" eventually were dropped as terms in the objectivists' psychological vocabulary.

HERMAN VON HELMHOLTZ (1821–1894) AND WILHELM WUNDT (1832–1920)

The character and limitations of psychological research and thinking in the late nineteenth century can be said to be characterized by the objectivism stemming from the Eighteenth Century, the theory of evolution (which was in that objective tradition), and a concern with consciousness that was more consistent with the Kantian influence. Von Helmholtz (Boring, 1950) was perhaps the outstanding biopsychological researcher of this period. He understood clearly the objective tradition but was sensitive to issues of consciousness. He made discoveries concerning the character of the central nervous system as well as the functioning of nerve fibers. One of Helmholtz's more interesting concepts was that of unconscious inference. Perception may contain experiential data that are not immediately represented in the stimulus. Any of the standard perceptual illusions serve as examples. He believed that extrastimulus elements contained in a perception were unconsciously determined, and called them "inferences." They are formed by experience and are irresistable in the subject. Well-established associations are virtually inevitable. An object is an aggregate of sensations formed in experience through sensations habitually occurring together. It is not analyzable into those sensory constitutents except by a special act of attention; that is, one can analyze the line-by-line perception of the common perpendicular illusion, but it does not account for the inevitability of seeing the baseline as longer than the perpendicular. This perceptual "interpretation" is what Helmholtz was referring to when he spoke of unconscious inference. In short, he recognized the incompleteness of directly objective sensory analysis.

In a similar tradition Wundt (Boring, 1950) insisted upon self-observation or introspection as the necessary method of psychology. This method presumably would capture that aspect of perception that was not includible in direct sensory analysis. Introspection was used to describe consciousness in terms of singular formal elements, which were connected by the principles of association. Wundt, like Leibniz, was also a psychophysical parallelist and concluded that mind and body cannot be directly compared. He essentially dismissed the body from psychology. Psychology dealt with the process of analyzing consciousness into elements and their laws of connection. Wundt believed mind or consciousness to be immediately phenomenal and thus not an object capable of being analyzed by other than its own principal process, namely, conscious introspection.

THE KANTIAN TRADITION

During the nineteenth century, particularly in the latter half, there were also scientists who followed the Kantian tradition. They utilized the concept of consciousness as the starting point for analysis. I have suggested that, by the twentieth century, consciousness was to drop out of the empiricists' vocabulary, although it would continue in the phenomenological tradition.

Some of the significant figures of this era were Hermann Lotze (1817 – 1881), Franz Brentano (1838 – 1917), Oswald Kulpe (1862 – 1915), and Edmund Husserl (1859– 1938). Husserl was, by far, the most important figure in the development of phenomenology. The concern of these men was to describe human activity in terms that would preserve the phenomenal quality of each basic perceptual process. The emphasis was on description, since a tacit assumption was made that thought or mind had certain specific characteristics that yielded immediate perceptual capabilities, independent of specific stimulus patterns that might be impinging upon it at any given time. They did not mean that experience via stimulation was irrelevant to understanding basic perception, but rather that certain characteristics were innate and could only be carefully described. For Herman Lotze, the mind is innately capable of arranging things spatially but separates out nonspatial materials to generate these spatial arrangements. Every tactile experience has its local signs. A touch on the skin has its own peculiar set of intensities since the contour of the skin is different all over the body. Being equipped with a large number of these local signs and knowing which of these signs are adjacent allows us to construct a kind of solid space. We do this because the mind tends to arrange all content spatially. The mind puts local signs together by utilizing bodily movement, and through this process psychological space is created.

Franz Brentano (Boring, 1950) focused on the psychical act in contrast to the content of mind that was important to Wilhelm Wundt and his students. Phenomena possess immanent objectivity when they refer to a content and have the object existing intentionally within them. Phenomena can be thought of as acts. Seeing a color is an act, not the color itself. A psychical act is not self-contained but contains its object (color) within itself intentionally. In contrast, a physical phenomenon is complete in itself. There are act classes such as ideating, judging, loving, and hating.

Edmund Husserl (1964) classified immediate experience into 1) phenomena —sensory and imaginary data such as tones, colors, and images which are the subjects of phenomenology; 2) psychical functions such as perceiving, grouping, desiring, willing — these functions are similar to Brentano's acts and are considered to be appropriate to the field of psychology; 3) relations; 4) immanent objectivity — sensory content and intentionality to see a color or to like a color. Husserl's work will be discussed in greater detail in Chapters 3 and 4.

Oswald Kulpe is an interesting figure in the history of psychology since he began as a content psychologist in the Wundtian mold and, based on his experiments on reaction time, changed his conception of psychology to emphasize the dependence of facts on the experiencing individual. The question arose among Kulpe and his students as to whether all attributes of the sensory impression are simultaneously present in consciousness since an individual's attentive predisposition may lead to a failure of introspection with regard to some attributes. For example, one of his students discovered that reaction time was different if the subject concentrated upon the key he was pressing in response to a flashing light, compared with concentrating upon the flashing light before pressing the key. Also, Marbe (another of Kulpe's students) noticed that subjects correctly judging weights could not tell how the judgments came to mind. The question then arose as to what other contents could exist in consciousness to account for thought when the images and sensations that introspection always yielded proved inadequate.

These doubts gave rise to the conception that there were four periods of attention in a psychical act. The first was the preparatory period which focused upon the task (*aufgabe*). The second was the appearance of the stimulus; the third the search for the reaction; the fourth the occurrance of the reaction. The first or preparatory period is of extreme importance. It was during this period that the subject sets himself for the task. (This concept of set or *einstellung* was later to influence the development of the concept of attitude, which became the central idea in the social psychology of the twentieth century.) To these act psychologists, it was clear that the characteristics of the stimulus and the immediate conscious characteristics of the perceiver were not sufficient to account for his behavior or conscious content. It apparently followed that a change in the set or the task might change the entire pattern of response. This observation was important to twentieth century Gestalt psychologists.

The act psychologists' position with regard to perception became the following: Form in space is a new quality. It is perceived immediately. Because the qualitites of the stimulus change without changing their form, there must be an independent form quality. Thus relations inherent in the nature of the perceived object were of central importance. Form qualities come as wholes in the perceptual act. Experience is usually given in great unanalyzed wholes, which attention to the parts destroys. A visual perception of form consequently depends greatly upon the attention of the observer, which is influenced by his sensations and images at the time. Thus, for Kulpe and other act psychologists, "function," "act", and "content" were different. Content can be analyzed in consciousness whereas function cannot be, because analysis alters function but not content. The method of act psychologists was to carefully describe certain perceptual events and then reason from these observations to others about the nature of human perception. They were empirical without necessarily being experimental and developed what was later to be called the *experimentum crucis*; a demonstration that presumably convinced one of a principle of perception immediately upon presentation. Thus, the example given above of a change in reaction time by altering the instructions to the subject would be taken as an *experimentum crucis* demonstrating the existence of a set in the subject. This became the principal method of Gestalt psychology.

WILLIAM JAMES (1842–1910)

Although James' (1962) contribution to psychology was extensive I wish, in this context, to emphasize his essential continuity with the act psychologists with whom he was contemporary. He was considered by many to be in the mainstream of the European phenomenological movement at the same time that he was imbued with American empiricism. Combining these two conceptual directions, he represented the best thinking about psychological activity in America at the time. As did the act psychologists, he believed that mind or conscious states are not composed of elemental units, but rather of states that an individual knows directly and concretely. In short, sensations are not the building blocks for higher states of mind, which are given directly to experience.

James also believed that psychology cannot question (as Mach did) the existence of personal selves. This followed from the idea that mind states are composed of units that are given directly to experience. The felt connection among these mind states yields a notion of self. James believed that the worst thing psychology could do was to interpret the nature of self so as to rob it of its immediate experiential quality. One is both aware of himself and is aware of being aware. The total self is duplex, partly known and partly knower, partly object and partly subject; that is, it is I who am aware of me. However, all mental states are accompanied by bodily activity of some sort. Mental action may be a function of brain action as effect is to cause, which James saw as the recurring hypothesis of physiological psychology. However, he realized that we do not explain the nature of thought by affirming this dependency. The principles of operation of thought may be different from the principles of the brain, even though one is a necessary condition for the other.

JAMES ON PERCEPTION

James was enough the empiricist to believe that experience is necessary for the activity of mind to act on the data of sense. Thus, every perception is acquired. James defined perception as the consciousness of particular material things present to sense. Sensations are modified by the ideas of mind. Thus the ideas of mind are a priori and are more powerful than sensations in apperception.

James's interpretation of reasoning followed from his position on perception. Our nonsensational conceptual states of mind present themselves immediately and refer to power beyond themselves, unlike sensations. Sensations can be doubted, but thoughts and feelings cannot.

By 1896, James had an ultramodern perspective of the basic epistemology of psychology. He believed that the deterministic assumption is merely provisional and methodological and that the assumption of determinism is therefore still open to discussion on a level other than the scientific. A psychologist who wishes to build a science must tacitly take the deterministic position. However, this does not imply that all human characteristics are amenable to such deterministically scientific methods. We see here that the epistemological ebb and flow of subject and object was still active at the turn of the twentieth century.

With James' work, the history of a certain phase of psychology closes and contemporary psychology begins. The twentieth century encompasses the development of psychoanalysis via Freud, behaviorism via Watson, Skinner, Hull, and others, Gestalt psychology via Wertheimer, Koffka, Kohler, and Lewin, and existential psychology via Husserl, May, Maslow, and others. Physiological psychology remains somewhat outside the ken of any of these four systems, although it overlaps them in general scientific methodology.

The intricacies of behaviorism, Gestalt psychology, and psychoanalysis have been well documented in a number of sources. We shall not repeat the effort here, as later chapters will incorporate the principal ideas of each of these schools into discussions of extant theories in four of the major subdivisions of psychology. Some attention, however, must be given to certain psychological views of the nature of consciousness incorporated into the thinking of the early behaviorists.

EARLY TWENTIETH CENTURY VIEWS
OF CONSCIOUSNESS

By the start of the twentieth century the psychological emphasis on contents of consciousness began to weaken. In 1885 Mach, as we have seen, already made an argument against the legitimacy of other than objective methods in examining human existence. In 1913 John Watson made the first definitive break with the conscious content emphasis of psychological research. In place of the study of consciousness he substituted the study of behavior. His influence, particularly in the United States, was enormous. Watson's argument against the study of consciousness per se was developed initially as an argument against introspection as the principal method of psychology. The introspective analysis of consciousness had yielded a great deal of controversy. The laboratories of different psychologists produced different conclusions about the same phenomena depending upon the theoretical bias of the psychologist. Discrepancies were essentially uncheckable, since they depended upon the introspection of the trained observer of each of the laboratories. In short, there was no agreed upon basis by which hypotheses could be tested.

In order to introduce a psychological method whereby consensus was attainable by psychologists working in different contexts, Watson suggested a focus upon the behavior of organisms, which would depend directly upon sense data. Thus, the occurrences in an animal of running, jumping, and eating were behaviors that psychologists in a variety of laboratories could agree upon. That is, they could see, hear, and therefore measure such activities in a variety of organisms.

Watson (1913) was careful to point out that his approach did not eliminate the fact of either the presence or absence of consciousness, however defined, but rather did change the problem of psychology to an examination of behavior. He believed that consciousness was not examinable by any method that would allow for definite conclusions.

Behaviorism, by focusing on sense data, thus avoided all forms of questions regarding mind and body connection.Thus, discussions of parallelism and interactionism were eliminated from the lexicon of psychology. Watson's behaviorism focused upon the characteristics of various stimuli producing certain responses, not upon the organism's experience of those stimuli.

Watson's behavioral approach immediately seemed to have strong possibilities for the examination of many problems concerning both animals and human beings. The acquisition of any number of motor acts could be examined through an analysis of input stimuli and output responses. The work of Thorndike and Pavlov had already awakened great interest among American psychologists in the process of motor and automatic learning. Watson realized, however, that in order for a behavioral system to reach its greatest impact, he would have to deal with those behavioral elements of human existence that seemed most intentionally connected to what was called consciousness. It was simple to classify speech as verbal behavior, but to explain its acquisition and use via a sensory motor system, as one could explain reflexive behavior, needed a great deal of imagination. He explained complex forms of speech, and therefore thought, by suggesting that these processes developed as faint reinstatements of the original muscular act of speech and that these were integrated into systems that respond in serial order via associative mechanisms. In short, thought was explained in terms of sensory motor processes in the larnynx. There was immediate criticism of Watson's sensory motor explanation of thought and no one takes the position seriously today, but the problem remains as to how to explain complex forms of thought and language in behavioral terms utilizing behavioral methods.

In his paper on behaviorism ten years after Watson, Karl Lashley attempted to extend the behaviorist's analysis of consciousness into problem areas where Watson had not gone (Lashley, 1923). The Watsonian model of the substitution of general behavioral method for introspection included a relatively simple notion of stimulus and response, input and output. Lashley, more sophisticated in central physiology, extended the behaviorist position by substituting more and more complex systems for the various complexities of consciousness formerly used by the introspectionists, such as subconscious, unconscious, foreconscious, and coconscious. He criticized the introspectionist position suggesting that, even after all analysis of consciousness is completed, there is still something left; namely, the very experience of consciousness itself, which is not amenable to verbalization or analysis. He claimed that this was a faith, and by his own introspection he could find nothing about himself that was not verbalization. Even, he said, were it to be true that there was a nonverbal, nonanalyzable component to consciousness, it would not, by definition, be amenable to scientific examination. Hence, a subjective science or philosophy of consciousness is impossible.

Although Lashley had not quite seen the point of phenomenological consciousness as expressed by, for example, Husserl, his point was well taken in 1923 and is still a valid one: namely, that science, in the sense of the examination of sense data via an objective method such as the experiment, is not appropriate for an examination of felt experience and therefore of consciousness. For a psychology struggling to become scientific, Lashley's points were important. It was necessary to cut away the older methods of consciousnesslike introspection, but in so doing, the problems that consciousness posed were also lost.

For Lashley, the elements of what was called conscious content are the processes of reaction to stimulation and are continuous with the spinal reflex. Thus, physical postulates about the nature of mind are as legitimate as they are when applied to the material world.

Finally, Lashley correctly concluded that the demand of the supporters of subjective consciousness that scientific description should be capable "of arousing the experience of the thing described [p. 347]" does not belong to the position of science but rather to that of art. He said that the psychologist cannot compete with the artist in a description of reality; the painter, musician, and poet are far better. This is true and is precisely the point at which phenomenologists such as Husserl and Merleau-Ponty found themselves in developing phenomenology, which ultimately is an attempt to carefully describe the world without theoretical bias.

It is noteworthy that while Watson eschewed any analysis of consciousness and therefore any conclusion as to its existence, Lashley attempted to substitute other terms and another analysis for the older forms. Tolman (1927) consumated this substitution by equating consciousness with decision making. He spoke of the "cause" of consciousness by offering the following definition: "Wherever an organism at a given moment of stimulation shifts then and there from being ready to respond in some relatively less differentiated way to being ready to respond in some relatively more differentiated way, there is consciousness [p. 435]." The moment of the shift is the moment of consciousness. Even complex cognitive differentiation may be an automatic process. The switch from one response to an entirely different one, or one idea to an entirely new one, defines consciousness. It is thus a process that is not given totally in the stimulus impinging upon the organism but does have a mechanical automatic quality.

By 1937, consciousness was no longer an issue among behaviorists. A consciouslike term "purpose of behavior" was utilized by Clark L. Hull. Organisms are seen to strive for goals or values and in so doing manifest a great deal of individuality with regard to their environment (Hull, 1937). However, at best, this purpose of behavior would seem to be causal in nature and therefore not different from causation as it is applied to physical entities. Hull attempted to solve problems of organismic behavior not only by using an objective stimulus and response analysis of behavior, but also by constructing a classical postulate system, which served as theory. Although not denying the existence of consciousness, he found that it would have added nothing to the terms in his postulate system, and indeed, was more a problem than a solution. He found no theorem whose deduction would have been facilitated in any way by the inclusion of consciousness as a term or postulate. Hull, like Lashley, correctly concluded that the idea of consciousness could not enter into a formal or semiformal scientific system.

2

A Selective History of Social and Motivational Concepts in Psychology

There are elements in the development of ideas relevant to psychology that are not ordinarily included in typical histories of the field, (e.g., Boring, 1950; Murphy & Kovach, 1972). People such as Machiavelli (1952), Vico (1961), and Nietzsche (1956a, b, 1966) are more often discussed in histories of sociology or political science. The legacies of Hume, Kant, Darwin, James, and others have contributed largely to epistemology and the nature of human sensation. Machiavelli, Vico, and Nietzsche might be said to contribute more to ideas about the social and motivational structure of human beings. Their efforts provided the way to the Freudian revolution and are therefore of particular importance to an understanding of the development of much modern psychology. In this chapter, I have selected a few of the key figures contributing the major ideational structures that led to Freudian theory. My purpose in choosing these people is, through specific examples, to illustrate the central core of a certain kind of thinking about the motivational and social basis of human existence that has developed over the last 500 years. Although there is still attention to method among these theorists, they are not consumed with the use of experiment or with direct physical and biological processes. Whatever insights they have generated have been a result of their systematic, but technically unaided, observations of the world around them.

NICCOLÒ MACHIAVELLI (1469–1527)

Machiavelli lived in a period of political turmoil, which created for him a need to seek a way of ordering his society. A kind of executive anarchy existed in that rulers of the various fifteenth century Italian city-states changed frequently and were constantly in need of attending to military or political attacks from their like numbers. The city-states had lost much of their possibility for developing benevolent rulers. Machiavelli saw clearly that the strength of a ruler lay in his ability to control his own populus as well as his ability to defeat other rulers. He never assumed that it was possible for the people to govern themselves in any elective or democratic sense and, indeed, this had never really occurred to anyone else before.

The question then became how to create order in the state by use of the ruler's two devices of control: punishment and reward. An examination of the histories of city-states and other civilizations led Machiavelli to conclude that punishment should always be severe, for if a minor punishment is inflicted the victim has the power to seek revenge. Rewards can be used to gain support of the populus, but only in small matters, and should be given only from a position of power, and then only to people who have experienced the power of punishment from the ruler. Through punishment lies the prudent use of leadership, and reward must be given only so that the recipient understands that it is motivated by largesse rather than by fear.

Machiavelli was wary of the inherent distrust of those who cooperate in a political venture. If one is thrust to power through the efforts of others, a suspicion is raised. The one made powerful distrusts the maker as possessing precisely those characteristics that are dangerous to him in his exercise of power: namely, manipulatory and persuasive competence.

Machiavelli saw that the organization and discipline of war were principal arts of the ruler. The cause of the loss of one's state was brought about by a contempt for this art. There are modern parallels to this position as, for example, is expressed in the oft-quoted, "The price of democracy is eternal vigilance." To this day, nations that are militarily powerful are those that are most influential in the world's politics. War remains the ultimate resort of political power.

THE CHARACTER OF MEN

Machiavelli abandoned traditional morality as a model for life because it is not achieveable within the framework of how poeple actually live. To be consistent with ideals in the face of those not so burdened with them is to fly in the face of what human beings are. One may fight by rule of law, as a man at his best, or he may fight by using force. Only men can achieve the first; beasts know only the second. However, since men find that the first is often insufficient, they must have recourse to the second. This theme, Machiavelli pointed out, is consistently reiterated in the history of the Western world. The education of Achilles by the centaur is prototypic. The legend of the centaur, semianimal and semihuman, indicates that a prince must understand and use both natures, for one without the other does not endure. It is often necessary for the prince to act against faith, charity, and religion in order to rule best, both for his own dominion and for the welfare of those he rules. He must adapt himself to the variations of fortune. He must be able to do evil if good is not possible. In doing evil, that is, in using force as would a beast, it is necessary to *seem* to have the qualities of mercy, faith, integrity, humanity, and religion. These will balance the force that is necessary by creating a sense of rightousness. This observation seems to describe accurately much political action in today's world.

MACHIAVELLI AND VIOLENCE

Although it has always been an especially Italian problem, the theme of the differences between illusion and reality is sufficiently universal to apply to many situations. Hence, the juxtaposition of force and goodness can be read as Machiavelli's perception of the organic relationship between order and violence (1972). Violence is both a part of disorder and of order. Violence becomes part of order when it is an arm of a dominant people (for example, the Romans). Violence becomes part of disorder when it is not part of law or part of a dominant people. Roman order was built upon the class conflict existing between nobleman and plebeian. The military integration of violence with civil life was taken to mean that direct physical coersion rather than material or economic force is central to the human condition. The integration of force and order brings social life close to nature in that there is the acceptance of the necessity of force as part of order. All forms of society produce violence, but some control it better than others. Human beings will behave in certain ways that are not always virtuous. However, it is virtuous to recognize that they will and must be this way because it is their nature. Machiavelli placed this conflict in the center of sociopolitical existence.[1]

The recognition by Machiavelli of the existence in all men of tendencies toward order and violence is the core of his political philosophy and is a recognition of the existence of oppositive qualities in man that were to be made central by Nietzsche and Freud. The sense of justifiable violence as displayed by the Romans was to be both the central point and the central example of Nietzsche in his concept of the superman.

GIAMBATTISTA VICO (1658–1744)

We shall see in Vico's work a continuation of the concept of opposites that Machiavelli saw as inherent in human social institutions and emotions. This concept of opposites comes from a theorist's sense of the dialectic inherent in

[1] There is some evidence that Ibn Khaldun, the Berber thinker of the fourteenth century, grasped this reality for Arabian people 100 years before Machiavelli (Becker & Barnes, 1952).

the structure of knowledge. Although a sense of the dialectic can impinge on any attempt at understanding, there is a dramatic impact when it is linked to social and emotional contexts. Vico extended and refined some key Machiavellian concepts. His work paved the way for others such as Friedrich Nietzsche, who brought the dialectic in a socio-emotion context to a chilling conclusion.

Vico's major work, *Principles of New Science of Giambattista Vico Concerning the Common Nature of the Nations* was initially published in 1725. In it Vico emphasized the human as opposed to devine origins of the state.[2] Though he invoked devine providence as the ultimate origin of human society, this providence took the shape more of original human nature than it did of ontology couched in theological dogma.

Vico followed the Cartesian lead in maintaining that an understanding of man begins with the metaphysics of mind. Hence, epistemology precedes examination of man as socius. By so doing, Vico eliminated the organismic analogy of the Greeks and of Thomas Hobbes as prototypic models of the nature of society. This allowed him to examine cognition, particularly language, (and, specifically, its history and structure) as the data from which conclusions about society may be drawn.

Vico's method of analysis was to reconstruct the development of early civilization by referring to its history and to the changing meaning of key words in a given language that refer to social, political, and legal institutions and customs. Etymology, therefore, plays a central role in Vico's analysis. His epistemological assumptions may be arranged as follows:

1. *Scienza* (knowledge or science) is characterized by philosophical inquiry and is a search for the True (universal and eternal principles). *Coscienza* means consciousness in the sense of awareness and is characterized by philological and historical search for the certain. While *scienza* is a search for eternal principles, *coscienza* is the observation and interpretation of particular facts, events, customs, laws, and institutions. Vico (1961) stated:

> Philosophy contemplates reason, whence comes knowledge of the true; philology observes that of which human choice is author, whence comes consciousness of the certain. This axiom by its second part includes among the philologians all the grammarians, historians, critics, who have occupied themselves with the study of the languages and deeds of peoples; both at home, as in their customs and laws, and abroad, as in their wars, peaces, alliances, travels, and commerce. This same axiom shows how the philosophers failed by half in not giving certainty to their reasonings by appeal to the authority of the philologians, and likewise, how the latter failed by half in not taking care to give their authority the sanction of truth by appeal to the reasoning of the philosophers. If they had done this they would have anticipated us in conceiving this Science [pp. 21, 138–140].

The separation of what might be called the science of basic principles from the ex post facto analysis of existing social structures had important implica-

[2]As had Ibn Khaldun (Becker & Barnes, 1952).

tions for problems in methodology and conception that arose later in the social sciences. Vico indicated that both approaches are necessary in developing an integrated picture of the nature of human beings. The interesting point in Vico's position from our perspective is that philology provides a necessary epistemological structure for understanding human social existence.

2. We can have science or knowledge only of what we ourselves make or do. We know about mathematics because we create the fictions that serve it. We know physics in that we do an experiment. Both fall short of complete knowledge because the objects of mathematics are fictions (abstractions not related to any real or imagined empirical object) and the physical experiment can never, even by definition, encompass nature as a whole. *Scienza* of the civil world, the world of institutions and customs, is possible for men because they (not God) have made it. Such a science can be both complete and real, unlike either physics or mathematics, *because* man has made it. It can be complete because it deals with the way man is and with the way he structures avenues to fulfill his goals and purposes. It can be real because it has to do with objects in the world and with other people. Its principles are to be found within the characteristics of our own mind.

Although Vico did not draw such a consequence directly, it is clear that he must have also held that it is not possible for experiments to be done that will yield valid information about man as socius. An experimental social analysis (social psychology, sociology) is not logically possible given Vico's assumptions. He believed a science of society can be complete and real because he saw it as largely separate from sciences like physics and mathematics. However, we may note that, to the extent that man is a physical being, he is susceptible to some of the laws of physics. That is, whatever the experimentally discovered biological truths are about man, they are not made by man and hence cannot include all of what is true about man as a social being.

3. Each nation (in the sense of a basic civilization; e.g., Greek, Roman, Hebrew) has an independent origin such that the same internal history is exemplified in each of them. It is interesting to note that this point is considered obviously incorrect and moot by Becker and Barnes (1952) in their book on the history of social thought, while it is the very point that is central to much of the theory of Carl Jung. Becker and Barnes explain as self-evident that nations influence one another in their fundamental development. Vico's contention is that if they are similar, it is because they have the same human problems, but are not necessarily influenced by one another. This Vichean assumption is a direct precursor of the Jungian collective unconscious.

While consciously pursuing their own ends, men everywhere have unconsciously served wider ends. The individual vices of people in socio-political power quite often yield public virtues. For example, the greed and pride of the Mafia yields a loyalty among its members that is enviable and is emphasized by the publicity given to the rare violations of this code. Rigidity, which accompanies violence in a leader, may yield a successful and desirable military discipline among citizens, if such a man is charged with the defense of a nation. The similarity of Vico to Machiavelli is evident.

The characteristics of nations did not come about by rational deliberation (as Hobbes had it) but rather by divine providence (which can be understood by the modern reader, who is uncomfortable with the theological reference, as human nature in its rational and irrational aspects).

4. It is of great importance to begin an analysis of human civilizations at their beginning and not with their modern counterparts. This is because modern states have the benefit of ideal justice and law as developed by the philosophers. The natural law of people (gentes), which was a law of force, can be examined best at the dawn of modern civilization. It is this natural law of the people that is most fundamental to and allows us to understand the nature of human society.

Vico was aware that this new approach to understanding society must be itself examined to discover where it began and what its nature is; in short, the sciences, and especially Vico's new science of institutions, are institutions themselves — products of human nature. It follows from this that science in general, and Vico's science in particular, partake of the initial divinations and auguries that were human beings' first attempt at understanding and predicting the world about them. Thus, one who would understand human social qualities must first understand the origins of social existence.

Legalization arises and develops because the character of human beings requires it so as to produce some semblance of order. From natural ferocity, avarice, and ambition, all of which are characteristic of the human race, the military, merchant, and governing classes are created. Out of these destructive passions, characteristics of individuals, civil order, and happiness are born.

Through the language of an ancient nation such as Greece or Italy it is possible to discover the customs of the early days of these cultures. The natural laws of the people of Italy can be understood through a philological examination of Latin. The same can be done for Greece and Germany. (Vico considered Greek and German to be the other two basic languages of eighteenth century Europe).

THE SYSTEM

Nations began in a savage state (already noted by Thomas Hobbes) and eventually developed laws. When a state became powerful and increasingly warlike, the laws no longer served to subdue the citizenry. Religion became the only powerful means to reduce the savagery of a population. It did this by awakening fear for an imagined divinity so that the people began to insist on some order among themselves. Human laws unattached to the conception of a divinity are unknown in the Western world. With this connection between divinity and public order, it is natural for nations to develop the concept of a hero who combines the qualities of strength, law-giving, and bravery. Vico points out that every Western nation had its Hercules.

The construction of laws accelerated the speed at which each language developed. The development of language interacted greatly with the development of social institutions and customs. Vico assumed that the changing structure of language reflected the changing structure of man and society.

The earliest thinkers, unable to use the complex abstractions of modern language, attributed senses and passions to objects quite often as large as the earth or vast as the sky. As the power of abstraction grew, these anthroporphisms diminished to mere signs. Thus from the mythologies of man, the qualities of earlier civilizations are communicated. Achilles is a sign for valor common to all brave men as Ulysses is a sign for prudence among all wise men. Metaphors arise in a language at this time. Every metaphor is a mythology or fable in brief. Vico notes that in all languages most expressions relating to inanimate objects are formed by metaphor from the characteristics of the human body: for example, head for top or beginning, the eye of a needle, mouth for an opening, the teeth of a rake or comb, the tongue of a shoe, a neck of land, the hands of a clock, foot for end or bottom, a vein for mineral. Man in his ignorance makes himself the rule of the universe. Rather than man becoming all things by understanding them, man becomes all things by *not* understanding them: (Vico, 1961): " . . . for when man understands he extends his mind and takes in the things, but when he does not understand, he makes the things out of himself and becomes them by transforming himself into them" (p. 88).

As an example of Vico's reconstruction of a bit of social history the following description is enlightening: Draco was author of laws written in blood (war) at an early period in Athenian history. Draco was one of the Gorgon serpents nailed to the shield of Perseus, which signifies the rule of the laws. This shield carried frightful penalities and turned to stone those who gazed upon it, just as in Christian history similar laws were called *leges sanguinis,* laws of blood, because of the harshness of the penalities they carried. The Chinese similarly use a dragon to denote civil power even though they are geographically separated from Greece by a great distance. Vico in noting similarities in the mythic structure of two distant and apparently very different cultures, used this information to support the point that all cultures develop some similar major characteristics, since all human beings must live at least some of the same experiences and therefore come to the same conclusions about them. By tracing the content of a myth from ancient legend to modern symbol, Vico demonstrated the socially informative nature of poetic mythology.

An application of Vico's etymological analysis follows: In ancient Greek "name" and "character" had the same meaning. In early Latin "names" meant houses branching into many families. The use of names in these ancient times, especially the passing of a name from father to son, was the right only of the nobles. In Greek, *nomisma* coming from *nomos* means money. In French *aloi* is money and *loi* means law. This indicates the connections among the rights of family distinction by birth. Power, law, and money (which is issued by the law) are directly related.

THE ORIGINS AND CHARACTER
OF WESTERN CIVILIZATION

Feral man was at first tamed by his father when he submitted to familial discipline. Later he came to accept the laws of the civil states by his acquisition of religion. The "second comers" to civilization were the plebians, who were brought under the control of the nobles by agreement to serve them for the protection the nobles afford. These plebians were vitual slaves before the development of the auspices. Marriage, and therefore the identification of the patronym, was denied the plebians and became in itself a mark of nobility. These plebs formed the first *socii* or society in the world. They were totally in bail to their lords. Finally, the plebians, after much travail, demanded and got the rights of the auspices especially ragarding marriage (connubium). When the demand was met by the nobles, the plebians had effectively ceased to be slaves and became citizens.

When a son may take his father's name, it paves the way for his taking his property also, and thus he gains the right to have his actions judged by the same laws as those existing among the nobles. Once having gained these rights, the plebians, Vico said, always seek to change the form of government and the nobles always want to keep it as it is.

The first agrarian law was the granting of rights and land ownership when people ceased to be wanderers and settled in the first vacant lands they encountered or could seize from others. The collection of these land grants became the first commonwealths whether of Greece or Rome or Germany. Once such commonwealths were formed, distrust and savagery was turned in large part outward toward the stranger or foreigner. Here, Vico anticipated some of the later analyses of Karl Marx.

Vico has left us with a literary and philological perceptivity that yielded a highly plausible and hypothesis-rich analysis of the nature of early Western man. Whether his analysis is true or not, in a predictive or theoretical sense, cannot be determined. However, his is an empirical analysis that may be examined against other philological and historical data, which may or may not support it. Some of his more interesting points follow:

1. The class confrontation between noble and plebian and the importance Vico attached to it certainly anticipated the labor movement and conflicts stemming from it, which began in the nineteenth century, as well as the socio-political revolutions that continue in force to the present day. Michelet and Marx were influenced by him.

2. The idea that all men live some of the same basic experiences and independently come to similar forms of law, justice, and custom, because they share the same characteristics, is an idea supported by the psychoanalytic theory of Carl Jung.

3. Connected to the second point is the notion that the mythologies of a culture reflect the nature of the origins and concerns of that culture as well as their basic characteristics. That is a point also embraced by Jung (1956).

4. The idea that man and not God is the creator of human society is one that has the status of being a virtual truism today and was a point of great importance in the eighteenth century.

FRIEDRICH NIETZSCHE

Although both Machiavelli and Vico concentrated upon human society both were well aware of oppositive tendencies in individuals that influenced this process. As we have seen, Machiavelli's focus upon the reasonable (human) and aggressive (animal) characteristics existing within humans led him to understand the socio-political situation of the day in terms of the interplay of these motivational bases. Vico saw a similar kind of opposition between noblemen and plebian in the history of civilization. Both theorists understood the cyclical nature of human dichotomies in motivational and social terms. Nietzsche concentrated upon what he thought were the deepest characteristics of human beings. Although he was interested in social contexts as much as Machiavelli and Vico, he was more psychological in his interests. In so being he provided enormous insights which were to culminate in the work of Sigmund Freud. Nietzsche, however, was also an unabashed ethicist. In this he differed greatly from the scientists and philosophers of his day. The fact of the mixture of ethics with insights of a more objective nature gives us a clue as to possibilities and, indeed, necessities, for the structure of psychological theory, which we shall discuss in some detail in the final chapter.

Machiavelli's study of political power and his insight into the complementary existence of aggression and cooperation in men led him to realize that the prince needed occasionally to do evil. This indicated that Machiavelli recognized the moral implications of the necessary political acts of a prince. Indeed, if it were occasionally necessary to do evil or perform a crime, it was nonetheless a crime. He simply believed that doing evil was absolutely necessary to do the things that man must always do. Nietzsche, appreciating this insight, attempted to build a metaphysics that would exclude both aggression and cooperation from the moral realm. In short, Nietzsche realized that the performance of evil, the act of aggression, or the act of cooperation could be beyond good and evil, beyond the morality of the day, or beyond any universal morality.

As we have mentioned above, Machiavelli's and Nietzsche's insights are very important for the psychoanalytic movement and constitute the initial underpinnings of a way of looking at human beings that has become relatively common in the twentieth century. These ideas exist in juxtaposition with moral systems that insist that it is possible to expunge a great deal of agression and violence from people, on the assumption that they are essentially capable of no aggression at all. During the course of this study we will examine the role that each of these positions has played in the affairs of men. Even incorrect conclusions can act as a catalyst in the course of human affairs. The basis for Nietzsche's social dialectic is contained in his analysis of the mythic Dionysius and Apollo.

DIONYSIUS AND APOLLO

There are two tendencies within human beings, one characterized by Dionysius and the other by Apollo. Apollo is the diety associated with the plastic arts such as painting and sculpture where order and a certain calm contemplation are the typical responses of the artist. Dionysius is associated with music which is capable of inciting emotion. Apollo is the god of reason, of science, of rationality of the pursuit of pure intellect and of the abstract. Dionysius represents the celebration of phenomenal man, of cooperative man, of man as he lives from day to day and as he plunges into the world around him. In ancient Greece, the Dionysian celebration was one of complete sexual promiscuity overriding every form of established tribal law. All the savage urges of the mind were unleashed on those occasions until they reached orgiastic proportions. Apollo is the opposite; he holds the head of Gorgon, which he has severed and which represents the subduing of the brutal and grotesque Dionysiac forces. Eventually, both dieties, and both urges in man, are recognized by the Greeks as living side by side and both gods are celebrated.

Nietzsche saw, as did Machiavelli, that the Apollonian consciousness of the Greeks was but a thin veil covering the Dionysian brutalities and licentiousness beneath. Apollo demanded self-control. In order to observe such self-control, a knowledge of self was essential. Thus, Apollo must be introspective, rational, and calm. In the subduing of the Titan fathers, Zeus and his brothers represented the suppression of Dionysian forces by the Greeks and the temporary control of Apollo.

For Dionysian man, analysis and understanding, with all its attendent doubts, eliminates the possibility for action. In order to act, it is necessary to create simple dichotomous catagories. With any decision made or action taken, the opposite undoubtedly has its merits. For the Dionysian man, no action can work any change in the internal conditions of things. From this state, art is born as it releases us from the terror of existence. This is the realm of wisdom from which the logical, the scientific, and the rational are excluded.

In *Beyond Good and Evil* Nietzsche (1966) said, "Behind all logic and its seeming sovereignty of movement, there stands evaluations, or, more clearly, physiological demands for the preservation of a certain type of life [p. 11, Section 3]." Nietzsche believed that a great part of consciousness was determined by instincts and that even basic philosophical positions were in part determined in the same way. He believed that the ideas of a philosopher were guided and forced into certain channels by his instincts. The value of an action lies in what is unintentional rather than what is intentional. He clearly indicated an unconscious motivation, which at its core contained the Dionysian qualities that he, in 1886, favored as a corrective for the Apollian world of his time. It is precisely this focus on the motivational quality of the unconscious that Freud, a few years later, was to seize upon. It is interesting that, although Freud appreciated Nietzsche (and one may surmise that Nietzsche would have appreciated the focal point of Freud's position), he (Nietzsche) would have violently disagreed with the end of therapy to which Freud put to use the ideas of unconscious motivation. The therapeutic corrections for guilt and sublimation that Freud suggested were consistent with the Judeo-Christian emphasis that Nietzsche despised. As we shall see, guilt played a major role in Freud's personality theory. It was precisely this guilt, characteristic of the modern nineteenth century democracies (developed from the Judeo-Christian ethic) that Nietzsche felt had led to the destruction of the free expression of the Dionysian spirit. Freud's response to the problem, on the other hand, was to deal with the guilt as it occurred in individuals, accepting at least tacitly the expectancies of the surrounding Judeo-Christian society.

Nietzsche viewed Christianity as a slave culture of the weak inheriting the earth. Rome, and later Europe, capitulated to it. At one time the Romans were the noblest and strongest people who had ever lived; however, they succumbed to the slave mentality of Christianity. Aside from the Renaissance when men awakened the classical ideas once again, the history of Europe has shown a steady Christianizing and democratizing.

Nietzsche, in his analysis of Christianity railed against its weakness and its self-torture. What he failed to understand was that it is necessary to explain why all of the Western world was in its grip. It could not simply be that the essentially weaker multitudes took power out of the hands of conquerors. Deception of some sort was needed and the deception had to be accepted by the strong. The implication is that some of the fundamental ideas of Christianity, such as the taming of the Dionysian self in man, was desirable to the weary warrior and that Christianity was the most palatable approach to this end.

Nietzsche's criticism of rational philosophers centered on their neglect of the Dionysian in human beings. He claimed that these philosophers posed as if they had come to their opinions through the development of cold, pure, unconcerned dialectic, as opposed to the mystics of every sort who he believed were more honest and more dauntless when they talked of inspiration and grace in coming to their conclusions. He believed that, at base, philosophers of all sorts did indeed have a kind of inspiration, or more often a basic desire of heart, that had been filtered and made abstract and thereby distorted. Consequently, Nietzsche rejected both the Kantian position, based upon categories of mind, and reductive material atomism or empiricism, which he believed was easily refuted as a general philosophy.

Still there is an overlap between Nietzsche's and Kant's positions. Both are phenomenological in orientation, both begin their positions with an introspective examination of perceptions and feelings. Nietzsche departed from this position by his emphasis on the immutability of certain native emotions in life as the fount of all existence. These could be best expressed by a total giving over to the drives, desires, and emotions of daily life that were sacrosanct, particularly if they were free from intellectualism and guilt.

Ideas like cause and effect are pure concepts in the sense that they are conventional fictions for the purpose of communications. They do not consitute explanations of anything. The inner self is not subject to causal necessity or to psychological determinism. An effect does not follow a cause, since there is no rule or law of cause and effect. We alone have devised cause and effect for each other as well as other concepts such as law, number, freedom, and purpose. Therefore, freedom and nonfreedom are illusory as characteristics of human beings. No question of whether man is free or not free should arise existentially. When we project the symbolic world of cause and effect into things as if it existed within them, we act as we have always acted, mythologically—the unfree will or free will is mythology. In real life it is only a matter of strong and weak wills.

It is interesting that some of Nietzsche's assumptions with regard to epistemological considerations of cause and effect are not unlike Kant's. Both reject the idea of cause and effect residing in the characteristics of objects. Both center the ideas of cause and effect, number, and so forth, in the individual. For Kant, this becomes the sine qua non of his philosophy in that it is a description of the way the mind works. Nietzsche, although he placed such concepts in the human being himself, took them to be mythological in the sense that they serve other more basic needs; namely, the satisfaction of emotions and desires through the exercise of power. He largely rejected the philosophy and psychology of his time, including the structuralism of Wilhelm Wundt, which was already becoming ossified.

The English psychologists to whom we owe the only attempts that have thus far been made to write a genealogy of morals are no mean posers of riddles, but the riddles they pose are themselves, and being incarnate have one advantage over their books — they are interesting. What are these English psychologists really after? One finds them always, whether intentionally or not, engaged in the same task of pushing into the foreground the nasty past of the psyche, looking for the effective motive forces of human development in the very last place we would wish to have them found, e.g., in the inertia of habit, in forgetfulness, in the blind and fortuitous association of ideas: always in something that is purely passive, automatic, reflexive, molecular, and moreover, profoundly stupid [Nietzsche, 1956a, p. 158].

Nietzsche declared that psychology had gotten stuck in world prejudices and fears. It had not dared to descend into the depths. In these depths Nietzsche expected that one would find savage emotions that really guided human beings in their daily existence. To understand the morphology of the depths of a human being would lead one to understand better the development of the will to power. Nietzsche was not aware of anyone having even attempted to do this in thought. It is roughly at this point in history, perhaps a few years later, that Freud and later Adler were to take up this gauntlet.

ON EVIL

"We think that hardness, forcefulness, slavery, danger in the alley and in the heart, life in hiding, stoicism, the art of experiment and deviltry of every kind, that everything evil, terrible, tyrannical in man, everything in fact that is kin to beasts of prey and serpents, serves the enhancement of the species, 'man' as much as its opposite does" (Nietzsche, 1966, p. 54). The intellectual and emotional submergence of these aspects of human beings as part and parcel of what is important about them is a product of Judeo-Christianity. It is during this Christian period that the sex drive was sublimated into love. This, of course, became a central idea to Freud some years later.

When sex became sublimated into love, the idea of sex unadorned with love became evil to the Christian world. So, said Nietzsche, is it the case that men of prey were seen as something evil when Christianity took hold in Europe. If we still look for something pathological as the motive force for a man of prey (for example, Cesare Borgia), we will not understand what is true about him. If we understand the beast of prey we can understand the man of prey. Borgia displayed what was most true about man in terms of his fundamental nature and acted as someone clearly beyond good and evil. But Borgia was an exception and Christianity more and more created a pathologically soft society where, as Nietzsche indicated, even those who committed crimes against it escaped punishment because it seemed somehow unfair to this disintegrating society. The giving as well as the receiving of punishment for transgressions against society was seen to hurt it more than the criminal act itself. In this manner, morality and timidity became fused. This condition has been brought about in society by the acceptance by Europe of what Nietzsche described as the soft class of Oriental religions. By the late nineteenth century, he saw that Europe was succumbing to a growing tenderness, and he saw in this the threat of a new Buddhism of which he clearly disapproved. Nietzsche was prophetic in this instance, for today we see not only the qualities of Judeo-Christianity of which he spoke, but the acceptance of far Eastern religions such as Buddhism by a small but visible number of young people in the West. The contemporary turning toward the occult is part of this movement. Nietzsche foresaw this and interpreted it as the increasingly degenerate portion of the Judeo-Christian inspired social democracy. The communist countries, which Nietzsche despised, although having similar herdlike political systems, have not yet developed to the point where they embrace strange or foreign religions as do the older capitalistic democracies.

One of the difficulties with Nietzsche's analysis is that although he condemned the democratization of the world he did not explain why so many countries have embraced some form of egalitarian government whether of the capitalistic or communistic variety. Why has virtually the entire world, over the past few hundred years continually moved in the direction of various forms of egalitarian political systems? I would suggest that one of the reasons for growing democratization of political systems, which Nietzsche did not see, has to do with the advance of technology initially in the West and eventually in the rest of the world. We will discuss this point below.

In contrast to the herdlike development of democratic institutions with power resting in large numbers of individuals, he speaks of a desirable supranational type of man who is beyond good and evil. The superman has essentially disappeared in Europe. Among the last few of whom, he counts Napoleon, Cesare Borgia, and Machiavelli. The passing of this type is the result of Europeans becoming more and more civil to one another and in this lies their weakness. A superman who is above this democratization can and will be a tyrant in every sense of the word including the most spiritual.

NIETZSCHE AND VIOLENCE

The Dionysian quality that Nietzsche sought to affirm as the basis of existence in the universe is a quality without value judgments, a quality beyond good, evil, and, therefore, violence. Destiny becomes important within this scheme. The Dionysian grasps the idea of an uncontroled destiny and enjoys it. Life is fundamentally nonorder. The negation of order is beyond anything real or conceived. It is a primitive state that must be grasped so that being and becoming can be seen to have no purpose or meaning. Therefore, being and becoming entail no guilt or merit, no intrinsic value or meaning. Having grasped this principle, action, creativity, and indeed life will eventually introduce a necessary movement that will entail violence. Power will enter into evil but not necessarily be a part of it (Polin, 1972). This is the will to power that we have seen in Machiavelli.

The best that issues from this condition of the world is a superman who is able to understand, feel, and utilize this Dionysian quality and to affirm life by being consistent with it. This Dionysian vitality in a superman has already appeared in the Athens of Pericles, in the Rome of Caesar, and in the Italy of the Renaissance.

The primitive nonorder of the universe is reflected, for Nietzsche, in the essence of man. This essence needs to be discovered beyond reason and beyond rationality. There needs to be a focus upon the emotions and the desires of human beings as they exist. This contention not only sparked the investigations of Freud but influenced later phemomenologists who were to begin their studies with similar assumptions.

The distortion of Nietzsche by the Nazis during the 1930s is, in part, their misreading of his affirmation of the conquering Aryans, examples of whom he took largely from Greeks, Romans, and Renaissance Italians. Nietzsche included all Europeans of a conquering nature under the rubric "Aryan" and associated them with anthropological likenesses in hair, skin, and other morphological characteristics. The Germans, at the time at which he writes, had not fulfilled their Aryan possibilities, as had the others. They had not yet seen their superman. It was relatively simple under the circumstances of his rise to power for Hitler to assume that it was the Germans' time to step into the place of the Greeks and the Romans. Unfortunately, what was maximized in Hitler's view was what Nietzsche probably would have called "the petty uses of tyranny and vices." [However, critics to the contrary notwithstanding, it seems impossible to conceive that Nietzsche would not have approved of a great deal of what went on during the Nazi regime in Germany.] To his credit, it must be said that Nietzsche despised the antisemitism in the Germany of his day as he despised Judeo-Christianity.

Nietzsche scholars such as Walter Kauffman and Ramon Polin become exercised when some treat Nietzsche as the inspirer of the Nazis. He certainly did not seem to be that, but at the same time there is a quality about the Nazis that is consistent with the Nietzschean position. They did identify Aryan characteristics among people by the physical qualities given them by Nietzsche's confused anthropology. (Most of the conquering Greeks, Romans, and Renaissance Italians who Nietzsche admired were not tall, blonde, and fair-skinned.) The Nazis did reject Judeo-Christianity with a vengence and tried to focus for their spiritual background on pre-Christian paganism, which was more consistent with the primitive nonorder that Nietzsche emphasized. It is clear that these were some of the more superficial characteristics that Nietzsche identified with the superman, but, although he might have been horrified with the result of this application of his philosophy, it should have not been unexpected.

Almost certainly, a modern application of some of Nietzsche's ideas on a large scale must result in a Hitlerian Germany or a despotism of some sort. One of the reasons for this is that modern technology allows power to reach the weak, a situation unlike that existing in 1886. This is particularly true as concerns the modern weaponry of warfare, which in 1886 could be considered rudimentary compared with today's ordnance. Even at that time, Europeans, by virtue of their technological superiority, easily overpowered non-Western peoples. If they overpowered one another, it was almost always a question of superior will, organization, or ferocity. It was during this time and before that one could imagine that a nation was capable of dealing with another success- fully in a military or political sense because it had supermen. Beginning with World War II in 1939, this was no longer possible mainly because some countries had far outstripped others (by Apollonian means!) in the technology of warfare. These imbalances accompanied changes in the attitude of the people, particularly toward war; for example, Germany easily defeated France in 1939 where it could not do so in 1914.

Those nations that were technologically advanced not only developed the peculiar technology useful for war or industralization, but also the ability to organize and order a large segment of life. It is one thing to invent the refrigerator; it is quite something else to organize the flow of raw materials from various parts of the world in order to move smoothly through the industrial process so that these machines may be mass produced and distrib- uted. These events shape the character of a society.

It is possible that today the world has became so democratized that the advent of despots such as Hitler are precisely what Nietzsche would have predicted. To imagine modern Western people developing that rock-hard quality of strength of being beyond good and evil is increasingly difficult not only because of the surge of democracy and the continuation of Christianity, but also because technology has weakened the need for a slave mentality as it has weakened the need for a master whose will to power drives the herd before him.

There is no doubt that Nietzsche was prophetic, particularly in his predic- tions that a democratized society comes to the point where it defends and feels pity for those whose acts destroy it, such as criminals. However, I would suggest that it may not only be the slave morality of Judeo-Christianity that produced this condition, but a technology that increases softness by providing people with necessities and luxuries beyond the wildest dreams of their ancestors. Among other things, the technology of modern warfare increasingly disallows a test of arms in any sense that can be identified with the individual himself. He no longer swings the sword or rides the horse with lance to battle.

Remote killing techniques now in existence among armies create a different type of warrior, a type which Nietzsche probably would not have appreciated.

Nietzsche's historical importance for psychology was his insight into the necessity of penetrating beneath consciousness to examine that aspect of human existence that was emotional, motivational, and primal. His notion that these factors were central in human existence and that all else was secondary was of crucial importance in influencing Freud. In short, he opened an avenue of human inquiry that had never really been opened before—an avenue that was to be walked by Freud, Jung, Adler, and generations of psychologists after them.

SIGMUND FREUD (1856–1939)

Although Freud knew and admired some of the work of Nietzsche, it is not clear how much he was influenced by him in the development of his own theories of human existence. From the Ernest Jones (1957) biography, one would have to conclude that it was little indeed. Freud considered Nietzsche great in his penetrating understanding of himself. However, Jones stated that Freud believed Nietzsche had not influenced him in any way whatever and that he had given up reading him because he found his philosophy so abstract and so unsympathetic. However, the similarity of Nietzsche's work to the psychoanalytic movement was sufficiently close for the Vienna Society to hold discussions of Nietzsche's writings in 1908. Freud did pursue Nietzsche's insights into the sense of guilt and the relief that people sought by committing some forbidden deed, the thought of which they then displaced, thus relieving this unbearable sense of guilt. Alfred Adler more closely followed the basic Nietzschean idea of the will to power and made this idea central to his form of psychoanalytic interpretation.

For our purposes, it is unimportant to establish whether Freud was directly influenced by Nietzsche's ideas. It is sufficient to indicate that he was aware of Nietzsche's work and that by the late nineteenth and early twentieth centuries the intellectual climate was such that men like Nietzsche and Freud, highly original in their work, could delve into the idea of an unconscious motivation in man, or in Nietzschean terms, a Dionysian man, that had at that time been buried beneath the Apollonian consciousness that had evolved. Of course, early psychologists, (e.g., Herbart) had made certain key interpretations of the unconscious and its influence on conscious processes, and this was available to Freud and his colleagues. It was not simply attention to the unconscious that Nietzsche provided Freud, but rather to the motivational, desirous aspect of it that was hidden from consciousness.

Herbart's influence on Freud (Jones, 1957) was distinct, but he was more influential on ideas about the process of unconsciousness rather than on the nature of its content. The conception of a continuity of unconscious and conscious processes, with the unconscious being the recepticle of motivations and desires that could not be brought to consciousness, was one of Freud's major insights. It also led him to conclude that neuroses are continuous with normal problems. Thus when one fully examined the unconscious, it would help to explain the advent of neurosis as well as the development of normal behavior. The idea of an active unconscious was readily accepted toward the end of the nineteenth century. In the beginning of the twentieth century it was questioned, as we have seen, by American behaviorists.

Nietzsche and Freud contributed important ideas to the concept of the unconscious. The unconscious is a repository for ideas and desires that are not, at any given moment, conscious. Freud held further that, because of the nature of some of these ideas and desires, bringing them to consciousness could be a difficult task for both the individual and the psychoanalyst. The unconscious was seen as the repository of the animal nature of human beings — the Dionysian self. Both ideas are, of course, related and Freud considerably developed and extended Nietzsche's initial ideas. The combination of Nietzsche's and Freud's contributions called attention to an aspect of human existence that had been neglected by psychology, but which was, clearly, of momumental importance. We will need to examine Freud's theory of the unconscious as well as those of one of his contemporaries, Carl Jung.

3

Phenomenology and Psychology

We have seen that the vision of the theoretician of human existence has been directed inward to the structure of his own thoughts and feelings or it has been turned outward to the processes of body and object in the external world. In cases where both foci have been incorporated within a system by the same thinker (for example, Descartes and Leibnitz) an epistemological separation between the two foci has been maintained.

The objective tradition embodies the idea that the object or event of study is to be understood as being acted upon by processes external to its indigenous characteristics. Scientists, in examining the motion of the planets, attribute no intelligence and therefore no terms of understanding to the planets themselves. The terms of understanding are attributed to human beings. The objective tradition would have it that an analysis of man himself, including his terms of understanding, should proceed methodologically in the same way that one would examine the planets or any other object. This places human beings in the position of having to understand themselves by using the tools created by their own understanding. An objective approach disallows the idea that the creation of the terms of understanding can emanate from the person as subject. The organism is conceived to be passive, in that no quality is uniquely attributed to it that enters into the explanation itself.

The learning of language has been described (Skinner, 1957) as a series of reinforced vocables. If, however, we constructed an explanation of the acquisition and use of language such that the capacities to respond verbally required the concept of cognitive dispositions separate from environmental contingencies, our approach would be "subjective." That is, if there are ways of thinking that are given in cognitive processes regardless of any *specific* activity to which an individual has been exposed, an explanation manintaining this premise has a subjective quality.

57

Most objectivists today, whether they be found in psychology or the physical and natural sciences, would agree that the objective tradition is all-powerful in dealing with biological and physical questions. Indeed, it may be epistemologically necessary to apply an objective approach to all areas of interest because of its general success in nonhuman realms. However, there are many questions about human beings for which the objective method has not provided answers. This lack of success can be attributed either to methodological and conceptual naivete or to the fact that the limits of the objective method have been reached in the study of human beings. The concepts that man uses to study himself are those that need to be explained in the first place. This is an epistemologically crucial point for psychology.

THE DIALECTIC

The dialectic has classically been regarded as a form of reasoning different from the demonstrative. The dialectic generally refers to discursive reasoning where meaning and truth are discovered by juxtaposing an idea with its opposite. This process of the constant opposition of ideas presumably yields meanings that were not previously apparent. Demonstrative reasoning refers to that form of argument that begins with "known" or "true" premises and extracts or deduces propositions already contained potentially in the premises. Modern scientific theoretical construction is of the demonstrative form of reasoning. These classical distinctions have often appeared along side of the subject – object dichotomy as methods of reasoning associated with each (dialectic and demonstrative respectively). For an extensive discussion of dialectic and demonstrative reasoning in the history of psychology, see Rychlak (1968).

As we shall see, the classical concept of the meaning of the dialectic was significantly modified by Freud, Jung, and others. I shall use this modified sense of the dialectic throughout the book. This modification focuses upon the thesis – antithesis opposition that is reflective of people as they actually live their emotional and cognitive lives. In short, the classical justaposition of dialectic and demonstrative reasoning is not emphasized. Indeed, the modern concept of the dialectic can, to some extent, be examined by the demonstrative process since it (the dialectic) is taken to be an observed principle of human emotional as well as intellectual functioning (à la Jung, see Chapter 6). Thus, the dialectic as a principle of argument is also taken as a more general principle of human functioning. (See particularly the discussion of Piaget's structural interpretation of mathematics for an analogous argument in Chapter 8.)

The objective position is well understood in America. The subjective position is not. It is often incorrectly equated with mysticism. We shall attempt to explain the human being as subject, particularly as it is presented in the system of Edmund Husserl and his followers.

Husserl's (1960, 1964) idea was to suspend all knowledge systems in order to discover what was most basically true about human beings and thus what information was available *before* these systems were invoked. We shall deal mainly with the ideas of Husserl and Merleau-Ponty, although I will not necessarily separate them in discussion.

PHENOMENOLOGY

For phenomenologists immediate experience is the starting point of understanding. Phenomenology examines that which is given (phenomena) in immediate experience before reflection on it emerges. Since immediate experience is perceptual and emotive, phenomenology, as all other basic human studies, takes the description of perception as its initial problem. The psychology of Hume and Kant and their later nineteenth century disciples was an attempt to discover psychological essences (basic qualities) or contents of mind (association of ideas, cause and effect). Phenomenology suggests that these essences must be examined within the context of existence. That is, a description of simple perceptual processes as they occur must first be made, since this immediate experience of the world epistemologically precedes essence. The difference between a phenomenological and a traditional analysis of essence and existence may be illustrated by the following example: If someone believes himself to be in love, there are certain feelings, thoughts, and emotions that he experiences. It is also true that both the individual and an observer can describe his state in terms of increased heart rate, changes in galvanic skin response, heart palpitations, and so forth, which occur in the presence of the loved one. There can also be an analysis of his behavioral–cognitive state at the time of his being in love. That is, he says he is in love and he extolls the virtue of his *innamorata*. It may be important to know about the behavior and cognitions accompanying this state of being in love. However, no matter what the analysis or by whom (an observer or the individual in love), the aspect of the situation that will totally escape analysis is the actual immediate experience of being in love: the experience of the emotions, thoughts, behaviors, and so forth, when they occur for the individual. That is, the state of being in love forever remains separate from analysis of it. Generally, in a consideration of all intense emotional states, there is little possibility of making an analysis of such a state which is significantly related to the experience of the state itself. When someone tries to describe love, it is often comic, so far is it from what people know it to be for themselves.

Psychologists have long recognized the differences between experience and an analysis of it, but have concentrated on the objective, analytical examination of various psychological and physiological states, particularly since the advent of sophisticated scientific techniques in the nineteenth century. During the nineteenth and early twentieth centuries, immediate experience was thought to be private to the individual and thus not part of what one could come to know in any systematic manner. At the same time, there have always been theorists (e.g., Brentano and Husserl) who have emphasized the possibility and, indeed, the necessity of examining the phenomena given from immediate experience as those closest to what is most important in life. Some believed that a careful examination of phenomena would eventually yield a proper basis for the emergence of objective scientific analysis of the same subject matter. Western thinking had, up to about the turn of the twentieth century, been diligent in its objective analytical approaches to human existence, but had lagged with regard to dealing with subjectivity. However, as we shall see, the development of psychology eventually required some attention to phenomena per se. "Phenomena" is the general label we apply to what is known immediately in consciousness.

Hence, phenomenology is a direct description of an object of experience while suspending (bracketing) any account of its psychological origins and the causal explanations applied by the scientist. Many of the best modern theorists of human nature, such as Nietzsche and Freud, are in part phenomenological, as we shall see. Thus, description is the general method of phenomenology as analysis and logic are the methods of most philosophy and science. For Husserl (1960) phenomenology is a return to dealing with the thing in itself, that is, an attempt to deal descriptively with experience and with objects as they are immediately experienced.

HUMAN EXISTENCE

A person is not the outcome of various causal agencies. One is but a bit of the world. All experience, including the scientific, is accumulated from an individual's particular perspective. Hence, science as an epistemology is secondary to phenomenal experience. To focus on things in themselves is to focus upon the world that precedes knowledge, the world of experience toward which knowledge is directed. It follows that not only science as we know it but analytical reflection or philosophy are excluded as possible methods to understand *direct* experience.

Analytical reflection begins with experience in the world and refers to the characteristics of the subject that are distinct from experience and that can be abstracted or summarized. To this extent, analytical reflection is not direct experience but instead provides a reconstruction of that experience. Also, my own reflection is aware of itself as an event. One must understand the operations of his own process of reflection and also recognize that this process of reflection is different from the actual event that it is dealing with. Ultimately, experiences must be described, not constructed or analyzed. This implies that perception cannot be placed into the same category as judgments, synthesis, analysis, or prediction. Perception is not statistical or probabilistic, or the perceiver would not experience the perceptual stability he does. Perception is the background from which all acts stand out and is presupposed by them.

One is not simply aware of existing. Rather, it is possible to distinguish things other than oneself, since an individual does not exist as objects exist. This notion implies an acceptance of the position of Descartes when he discovered that *cogito ergo sum*. If thought yields existence, then those things that are imbued with the ability to think are unique from those that do not have this ability. The resulting cogitatio has a phenomenal existence. Thought is an irrefutable fact. Thus, the world itself is not one-to-one with the scientific or traditional philosophical meaning of the world. If one accepts that before explanations of a traditional philosophical or scientific sort can begin there is plain existence, which is the stuff from which all knowledge systems evolve, this will influence the manner in which one approaches meaning and knowledge.

We enjoy direct access to what consciousness holds as an idea. This direct access to the world comes through our perception. If this perception is subjected to philosophical or scientific examination, we lose what we directly perceive about the world and ourselves. Even language itself, being of a symbolic and abstract nature, separates one from direct experience.

Phenomenological reflection attempts to emulate the unreflective process of consciousness. The world is what we perceive. To wonder if what we perceive is *the* world or *a* world is to already have left immediate, real experience and to have fallen back on analysis and abstraction. This position categorically removes the Humean difficulty of wondering whether what is perceived is truly what is characteristic of the object. That is, it is only the objective philosophers and psychologists who are confused about whether or not perception is perception of the world or a characteristic of the perceiving individual. Hume, Kant, and others became embroiled in this problem because they conceived the process of perception as separate from objects in the world and treated perception as if it has characteristics like scientifically analyzed objects.

Hence, for phenomenological psychology both objects in the world and the process of perception itself are immediately given and are not to be doubted as to their validity. The implication is that the perceptual process includes the apprehension of objects in the world. They cannot be separated. The nineteenth and twentieth century psychophysicists spoke of illusions because they had identified certain perceptual phenomena as having a purely physical, objective character. For example, the Muller−Lyer lines are neither equal nor unequal. It is only in the objective world that this questions arises. Another example is provided by the idea that the abstracted notion of distance is different from the experience of it. The phenomenological idea is that distance comes from relationships of tactile positions of the body. Feelings in thumb and first finger do not significantly show the relationship between points and space unless they were already situated on a path running from one to the other. Unless this path is not only transversed onto one's fingers as they are opened, but is also encompassed by thought pursuing its purpose, one cannot know the significance of a sign that he has not himself created. Self-consciousness is the very essence of mind in action. Perception is inseparable from this self-consciousness. In short, to see is to see something. Hence if one is interested in, for example, touch, it is the experience of it that one should be describing as *primary* rather than the mechanical and physiological processes involved in the depression of the skin, since this misses the point of what perception truly is.

Finally, it might be said that perception is not assessed truth, but truth in itself for the individual. The world is not what one thinks about it but what one lives through (Merleau-Ponty, 1962). This is also a rejection of the noumena–phenomena distinction of Kant. Our relationship to the world as it appears within us is not an object that can be any further classified by a scientific or philosophical analysis. Philosophy and science can only place this relationship before us once again for our perusal after it has occurred. This is precisely what traditional psychoanalysis does for the patient. It places one's relationship to the world as he has lived it before him once again without comment. Guilt and fear must be resolved or dealt with by the individual through his own phenomenological reality. Thus, phenomenologists see the process of psychoanalysis, but not the theory, as phenomenological in nature and Freud was really the first psychotherapist to utilize a distinctly phenomenological technique for therapy. We will discuss this and related questions in greater detail below.

It is clear from the phenomenological position that the subject – object dichotomy does not exist as a problem. That is, subject and object are fused by the phenomenological position. The only preexistent logos is the world itself. Consequently, the eighteenth century philosophical problems of differences between noumena and phenomena, or of differences between subject and object, or of the difficulty of discerning the world from a subjective self, are all exposed as nonproblems.

The first experience of the senses is understandable in the preobjective realm. That is, in the phenomenological arena, before objective analysis begins we are subject to meaning in that sensations and images, which are the beginning of knowledge, make their appearance within a context of meaning. This is indeed a significant percept in that associations of sense data in the Lockean or Humean sense may be presupposed. Perception inaugurates the foundation of knowledge and is not explained by it. Sense perceptions of our own body and the perception of external things is a cognitively constructed determining factor external to its effect. Therefore, perception cannot be assimilated by objective thought. Gestalt or any psychology is circumscribed within the concepts of science and can thus only use reason and causation in dealing with preception. Consciousness is not a collection of forms as the Gestalters would have it nor is it a series of objective relationships existing among elements of body or mind (thought).

Thus, for phenomenology, philosophy and science are suspended; they are knowledge systems, they are pursuits of the essence of phenomena. They are not attempts to deal with phenomena per se. It follows that there is also a rejection of the idea that human beings are the result of a series of causes; that is, of being a causal nexus. This does not mean that the idea of cause and effect is meaningless when used to refer to the activity of human beings. It does mean, however, that it is irrelevant to understanding the most important aspects of human existence. This position also implicitly questions the nature of learning. It rejects the Anglo-American interpretations of learning and the conception of some theorists that the process of caused learning is primary in human existence.

One of Husserl's major concepts is that human beings are a bit of the world, ebbing and flowing with it. The problem has always been that they have had the capability of abstraction and have tended to eliminate this aspect of themselves as being part of the world. That is, an organism capable of thought gets confused about its own organization. It finds that it makes causal conclusions. People, therefore, assume that they are products of many causes. If one brackets this knowledge, if one discovers he exists in the world immediately as he lives moment by moment, day by day, then some of the problems that are brought about by abstraction, like how can one both be the result of a cause and the creator of one, disappear. Some of the problems explaining the essence of what people are, are false in the first place, because the ability of humans to abstract turns back on itself (e.g., the discovery of the "blind spot" discussed above). This also eliminates the Kantian dichotomy of phenomena and noumena. It was only through the abstraction and separation of subject and object or mind and body that the problem came about in the first place. Phenomenology, going beneath abstraction, eliminates the problem because one is self and object in the world at the same time. Immediate experience involves objects in space, that is, through the experience of seeing, hearing, and touching.

The Humean and Kantian positions lend themselves to the development of the idea that self-existence and the existence of objects other than self are doubtful. This takes the form of doubting that one can, with surety, know that a sense impression really reflects something that is true about an object of its apprehension. This doubt arises naturally enough because Kant separates, as part of his assumptive base, objects in the world from self, and for Hume the individual has the same status as objects in space. Consequently, if there is some doubt about the correspondence between sense impression and the object perceived, as there frequently is, the entire process is in doubt. Avoiding this dilemma by establishing that self processes are certain but object processes cannot be certain (Kant) establishes doubt about the existence of the world outside of self.

As is perhaps obvious, the process of doubting is a natural consequence of the separation of self from the world in the first place. Actually, in any theoretical system in psychology there are no terms, procedures, or concepts that allow one to prove or disapprove one's own existence. To ask someone to demonstrate existence in an empirical or logical manner is to already be in the grip of an abstracted system that requires it. Another way of saying this is that when an individual believes causality to be central to understanding, he must deny his own existence because it cannot be demonstrated causally. This is abstracting ability gone beserk.

In summary, part of what the individual is is the object it experiences. Object and experiencer are both part of the world—they ebb and flow together —they are essentially inseparable. Hence, there is no doubt about the existence of the object because there is no way that the organism exists without objects (including itself).

The meaning and essence of objects are described by us. What they really are is intended (given meaning) by us. We immediately know of their existence. Therefore, there is nothing that would indicate that they do not exist when we do not intend them.

FREEDOM, DETERMINISM, AND CAUSALITY

Many phenomenologists consider that man is totally free. In order to be determined by an external factor it is necessary that one be an object or thing. Since human beings are perceivers and cognizers while objects external to them are not, it follows that they are free. I am free to posit another person whose consciousness penetrates my own existence. There is a restraint on freedom, however; the initiatives of freedom itself set its limits. If I say a stream is uncrossable, this belief is set from a desire to cross it. Thus freedom has set a limit to its own expression.

The concept of probability as applied to human activity is also rejected as a basis for its understanding; that is probability analyses that usually accompany the conclusions of a variety of psychological research do not deal with immediate experience since they are abstractions. Consequently, for the phenomenologist, probability analysis has the same epistemological status as a causal analysis and is equally rejectble on that basis. However, as we shall see in our examination of the system of Merleau-Ponty, there is a phenomenological basis to statistical thought as there is to science in general.

This concept of phenomenal freedom, if held as a proposition by a clinical or social psychologist, will influence the way he does therapy or analyzes social situations, respectively. Within the therapeutic context, a phenomenologist might say that a patient is committed to living with the idea of his inferiority and has done so for several years. Only a free act on his part can get him out of it. The therapist's role would presumably be to convince the individual, or to have him convince himself, that freedom is indeed possible. Since we are born into the world and of the world, there is neither a determinism nor an absolute choice available to us. For example, psychoanalytic treatment does not cure by producing direct awareness of the past in the patient, but instead binds the subject to the therapist through new relationships. The patient sees his part in the perspective of his coexistence with the therapist. Analytic therapy, although not theory, resists explanation through the application of experimental techniques because it is an immediate, perceptual situation whose major characteristic is that it must be lived through to be effective.

Merleau-Ponty has concluded that revolutions are free acts of workers deciding that they are members of an oppressed class and are not determined by objective conditions such as low salary or long hours. Thus, a proletarian is formed by internalizing within himself economic and societal institutions. An intellectual becomes a revolutionary by a different course. His starting point is his intellectual center; for example, he becomes convinced of the tenets of Marxism. For this reason, intellectuals are almost always suspected by proletarians although they are ostensibly in the same camp. The decision to become a Marxist is constructed in the course of the life of a worker. In an intellectual, a decision for Marxism can be the result of a cognitive exercise.

However, there is a distinct sense in which human freedom must be viewed as having its origins in a deterministic context. Human beings are products of genetic structure, the characteristics of which are independent of any choice they can make. It is perhaps sufficient to indicate that human beings biologically produce other human beings and not horses, and that they have little choice in the matter. Initial individual existence, whatever its characteristics, does not involve any choice. However, even with restraints, there is no indication that any given behavior is determined by a specific causal chain of events. The fact that human beings can interpret their activity as being caused or free illustrates the difficulty in deciding whether any given choice is determined or freely made. In short, the determinist's position is restricted by what is true about immediate experience, and freedom of choice is limited by the physics and biology of human existence.

In any case, it is not possible to *prove* the existence of freedom or determinism. The determinist can always fall back on his faith that a causal line will be found even though one is not immediately apparent. The believer in freedom can always maintain that there was a free act somewhere beyond an established causal line if one knew where to look.

Perhaps the important conclusion is that making an assumption of freedom or determinism is unwise. It is legitimate to search for caused human behavior. So long as this sense of determinism is restricted to the methodology and epistemology of the search for a *particular* answer. On the other hand, it is legitimate for someone to assume that human beings may make a free choice when conscious cognition is involved. In either case, of course, errors will be made. Usually, at least at this time in America, the error more often occurs with the theorists who would make a pervasive, if implicit, assumption of determination, rather than those who would make the assumption of freedom.

INTRODUCTION TO THE PHENOMENOLOGY OF MERLEAU-PONTY

No other phenomenologist has been more aware of the traditional problems in the psychology of perception than Merleau-Ponty (1962, 1963). He followed Husserl in his belief that a phenomenological analysis of perceptual phenomena is the initial problem for a phenomenological psychology and a phenomenological intuition. Phenomenology is to psychology as geometry is to natural science. Psychology is a science of fact and realities (phenomena). Pure phenomenology is the science of essential being (as against psychological phenomenology). Essential insight is intuitive. Sense experience is consciousness of an individual object which, because it is immediate and intuitive, brings meaning (giveness) to the object as perception. Consciousness immediately apprehends an object as it is in the world without any special act of analysis. On quite similar lines, essential intuition is the consciousness of something, but not about something (since this would imply a psychological phenomenology), something "self-given" within an object that can be made the subject of true and false predictions.

BASIC PERCEPTION

The influential theory of perception to emerge out of intellectual concepts extant in the late nineteenth century was that of Gestalt psychology.. This theory began with the observation that the perception of a figure on a ground is immediately given for the organism; that is, figure and ground have no contingent properties. Since the homogeneous field yields no perception, one would not have perception at all without beginning with the fact of figure and ground. The lack of contingencies in this relationship coincides with the general phenomenological contention. The same can be said of other types of basic perceptual phenomena. As we have seen in the Muller–Lyer illusion, the two straight lines are not of equal or unequal length in the phenomenal world of perception. It is only in the objective world that this can arise; that is, by laying a ruler beside each line, it is clear that the two lines are of equal length although they do not appear to be equal perceptually. The fact that this was labeled an "illusion" indicates that late nineteenth and early twentieth century perceptual psychologists implied that perceptual phenomena depended upon contingencies that coincided with the mensurative properties of the physical world. If one instead *begins* with the "illusion" as a consistent property of perceptual phenomena that is true of the perceiving constituting subject, no reconciliation is necessary.

Quite often, in the past, perceptual theorists needed to invoke concepts that would reconcile discrepancies between the mensurative aspects of the physical world and the perceptual phenomena added to them. One of these concepts was that of attention. Attention was invoked in order to explain the clarity of perception of one aspect of a field rather than another even though, given the physical characteristics of that field, all aspects should have been equally perceived. Since a phenomenologist does not make the initial objective assumption about the physical aspects of a field and its relation to perceptual phenomena, the concept of attention is not needed.

The traditional telephone switchboard interpretation of perceptual phenomena where there is an origin, a process, and reception area also is rejected. In any case, this model could not explain even attention or the perceptual constancies. Even the law of constancy refers to perception as it initially occurs and not to any experience in which it is not already implied. Wherever it is applied one will find that it is already presupposed. Perceptual phenomena are not constructed of the passive reception of the content of the external world; rather, the external world is constructed by perceptual phenomena.

Although it is true that the sensible is what is apprehended with the senses, this is not a simple relationship. That is, the sensory apparatus is not a conductor but is part of the central processes that in turn can only be understood as participating in the constitution of reality by the subject. In short, the phenomenology of perception cannot be forced into categories that are meaningful only in the universe of science. An isolated objective line and the same line taken in a figure are perceptually not the same. Sensations, which are the core of knowledge, always appear within an association.

ASSOCIATION

The traditional position taken by the British empiricists regarding the doctrine of association has made the laws of association, such as continuity and resemblance, determiners of a perceptual or cognitive condition that constitutes the content of mind. Phenomenologists such as Merleau-Ponty reversed this order. It is because we perceive cognitions and perceptions as things that an analysis of them can discern presumed laws such as continuity and resemblance; that is, principles of association occur to individuals after they have perceived the objects of perceptual processes as wholes. The phenomenon of the upside down image that is projected upon the cortex from the visual apparatus is a case in point. Psychologists long wondered why we saw things right side up when they were projected upside down upon the retina. Eventually they concluded that there was no right side up or upside down in the visual apparatus. This lends support to a noncontiguous, nonsensationistic interpretation of this and other similar perceptual phenomena.

The associationist interpretation of the nature of perceptual phenomena was codified by the logical positivists of the Vienna school in the early twentieth century. For Merleau-Ponty this codification reversed what is clear and what is obscure. The positivists interpreted immediate experience to be the obscure bit of data, and abstractions about experience to be clear data, whereas in reality Merleau-Ponty concluded that the opposite was true. The action of stimuli on our body is the final derivative of knowledge, not its inception. The abstract abilities of the mind and the idea of time leads us to think of sensation as anterior to knowledge. Perception is a judgment and as such is unaware of the reasons underlying its own formation; that is, the perceived object presents itself as a totality before we have apprehended any laws governing it. There is also an empirical or second-order (scientific) perception, which is present for every moment and which can conceal from us the more basic phenomena of which we have just spoken, because it is laced with earlier acquisitions of methods and abstractions.

For Merleau-Ponty, the making explicit of the prescientific life of perception alone endows scientific operations with meaning. A Gestalt perception is the appearance of the world for a perceiver and not a condition of its possibility. It is the birth of a norm and is not something that, taken together with other perceptions, yields a norm. It is the identity of the external and the internal and not the projection of the internal onto the external or of the external onto the internal.

As clear as it is that immediate experience must be dealt with on its own terms, it is also clear that any thought about immediate experience can never really be other than inductive or deductive. That is, the whole texture of any experience cannot be assimilated in thought. It is, however, possible for there to be an apperception of the phenomenon of the phenomena. In short, one can experience analytic reflection as a phenomenon in its own right. As we shall see below, this will lead to a somewhat different interpretation of the nature of science and other forms of analytical reflection than are given by many philosophers of science.

BODY PERCEPTION

The individual imbedded within an analytical mode of existence would be temporarily unaware of the possibilities of his immediate experience regarding his body as one of the objects of the world with the epistemological characteristics of other objects. It is possible, when one is aware of seeing, to consider one's eyes as bits of matter. Hence, they become objects with the same status as those that they apprehend. An object is an object when it can be moved from our field of vision; however, the permanence of one's body for himself represents an entirely different situation. It is always presented to one from the same angle. Its permanence is not universal but an object permanence that remains marginal to all of one's perception. It is *with* one rather than before one. Implicit within the fundamental perception of figure on ground is one's own body, which is the always-present third element. This permanence is a means of interaction with the world. Thus, the world is a horizon that latently permeates all experience. Cartesian and eighteenth century thought held that the body was not a phenomenon but a fact derivable from determinants. They believed that the mind was a phenomenon. The union of the mind and the body is the beginning of knowledge and does not need to be fused by analysis of any kind.

The body is a vehicle of being in the world and is therefore the means by which an individual is involved in a definite environment. Individuals identify themselves with a variety of projects and are often continually committed to them. This involvement in the world allows one to acquire the mental, practical space which can theoretically free him from this environment and allow him to *see* it.

Explanation in psychology as in any other field is never given with the objective fact, but is a probable interpretation of the nature of that fact. Explanations are not made by identifying commonalities among collections of facts. Explanation is created by the individual in the world. Although this is true in physics, for example, as well as psychology, problems are more acute in the latter. In psychology, the process of creating explanation is often directed toward the activity of psychologists themselves, which increases the difficulty of the task. Hence, phenomenologists reject explanation in psychology as an expression of the relationship of a function to a variable. For example, a stimulus is not the cause of a response but becomes its intentional object, in that the individual in the world brings as much of what he is to it as it does to him. In short, a stimulus cannot be conceived of as a cause nor as a preceding contingency to a later response. The intention of the individual regarding the stimulus is always present, except in situations where spinal and other reflexes are operative. Since human beings are capable of being conscious about the starting and ending points of any number of movements, they know where their body is without having to look for it as one looks for an object moved from its place during an absence. Therefore, Merleau-Ponty concluded, consciousness must either be denied altogether or it must be accepted as permeating all existence.

One can, with the idea of the number six, the idea of side, and the idea of equality, write a formula that is the definition of a cube. This definition puts a question to us rather than offering us something to conceive. Abstraction is penetrated by perceiving the particular spatial entity that links the terms of definition. The definition through abstract reflection gives us the idea of an absolute object rather than the absolute existence of the object. Conceiving of the object from no subjective point of view destroys its internal structure. Apprehending the cube means delving into the space of the world by perceptual experience. Hence, perception is a constant recreation of the world during every moment. It is not in itself an event in the world. Hence, causality is not a category that can be applied to it. The implication is that distinctions between the a priori and the empirical, and between form and content or between mind and body, must be eliminated.

Because the body image is always an immediate perception preceding abstractions about it, the perceptual synthesis of body and object no more isolates the object than it does one's body, and this is why the perceived object always presents itself as separate from the perceiver and why the synthesis seems to take place at the object in the world and not at the conceptual point occupied by the perceiving subject. Perceived consciousness yields the constitution of the world realized by the subject before the ideas of shape and size come into being. Kantian categories of mind, whatever their validity, are epistemologically derivative from perceptual consciousness and not the other way around. It is because I perceive the table with a certain shape and size that I assume for every change of distance or orientation a corresponding change of shape and size and not the reverse.

BEING

There are two modes of being — being in itself, which is that of objects in space, and being for itself, which is consciousness. It is clear from these modes of being that the perception of another individual is not classifiable under one mode or another. Another individual does not exist for us as an object such as a table or chair, nor is an individual totally part of our consciousness. Another person does exist for us as an individual himself and yet also in that he perceives that he exists for himself. Consequently, I both place another individual in the world of objects in order to distinguish him from myself and in the world of consciousness.

How is this possible? I deal with objects through my body and my body is dealt with through objects not in terms of logical derivatives, but because my body is a movement in and toward the world and the world is my body's support. If I thus experience this inhering of my consciousness in my body and in its world, the perception of other people and their consciousness no longer presents any difficulty. Of course, we distinguish between the objective body and the body that is capable of being inhabited with a consciousness. (Incidentally, we do not know how meaning and intentionality has come to develop in molecules and masses of cells. No science or philosophy that excludes the concept of God even attempts to answer this question.)

This contention is supported by the observation that the perception of other people is not a problem for the child. The child lives in a world that he believes is accessible to everyone. He has no awareness of his own or of other private subjectivities. He believes everyone is subject to one world point of view. At about age 12 he discovers himself as a point of view of the world and that he is expected to transcend that point of view to construct a judgmental objectivity.

FREEDOM

It is clear that no causal relationship is conceivable between the subject and his body or his world or his society. One is, for himself, neither envious nor hunchback nor a civil servant. It is often surprising to others that a cripple can put up with himself, but he is all that he perceives and is, and enjoys at least this much of existence. In order to be determined by an external factor, it is necessary that an individual should be a thing. Since it has been established that human beings cannot be things, all of their actions are free.

Besides rejecting the idea of causality in human affairs, motivation is also rejected. An alleged motive does not force a decision, on the contrary, a decision lends the motive its force. It is true that there are many abstract decisions made in the world that seem to involve motives and passions, but in these cases a choice has usually been made to be bound by what one discerns is his own motive structure. That is, it is an argument in bad faith to say that I can do nothing about my economic situation because I am oppressed by more powerful people than I am. Although I may not be able to change my economic condition directly, I can certainly freely choose to struggle against those who oppress me. In short, a true freedom exists between a whole, total individual and his manner of being in the world. Our choice of ourselves can be a conversion involving our total existence. It is freedom that brings into being the impediments to freedom, as we have seen above, so that the impediments set the bounds for the freedom. Here we speak of decisionary freedom. We have already discussed the biological limitiations of human possibility.

Although, as we have seen above, the concept of probability as a way of describing causality in human activity is rejected, there is a phenomenological basis for statistical thought. If one has committed himself to a way of being in the world for many years, it becomes improbable that he will change that commitment at present. But, as should be clear, this becomes an abstracted decision of the choice of quality of life.

Determinism is dependent upon the constituting activity of the subject. Freedom may be something implied in a free choice of seeing one's life as determined. Commitment sustains one's power in life and freedom always carries power with it. Because we are involved in the world and with others in an inextricable interaction, the idea of any situation rules out absolute freedom equally at the beginning and at the end of our commitment. The restriction to a commitment is having made *it* rather than some other. But in having made it, our power increases in that we have made a free choice and can do so again.

CONCLUSION

The phenomenological position as exemplified by Merleau-Ponty is an attempt to convince that it is possible to directly apprehend immediate experience. The fact that the effort was made at all implies that Merleau-Ponty believed that individuals are typically not aware or capable of understanding the centrality of immediate experience. His description is about what is potential in the apprehension of individuals, who, although they do experience directly, do not always realize that they do. As we have seen, Western civilization has imposed upon us a tendency, particularly through science, to separate our immediate experience from abstractions about it. Over the years, this came to us in the guise of the mind–body, subject–object, and nature–nurture separation. Phenomenology is an attempt to correct our tendency to think causally, rather consistently, with regard to our own experience so that we do not lose what can be seen in it. We are led to thinking that human beings are the result of a causal nexus of events because we have the tendency to abstract so readily about our experience. There was a period when many believed that a human being had a vast range of free choices. Because this idea encompassed the idea of God, it suffered all the difficulties of that notion. This was unfortunate since the idea had its own merits.

So often in emphasizing an aspect of being that is apparently opposed to that which has been emphasized to that point, a polar shift in thinking takes place. This results in the baby going out with the bath water. If causal thinking is at one time emphasized and one is convinced that a focus upon immediate experience is more fruitful, there is a tendency to downgrade the validity of causal epistemology. Fortunately, Merleau-Ponty pointed out that abstract thinking itself is a phenomenal given. Consequently, it is possible to describe the nature of abstract thinking through the phenomenological methods, which I shall do in Chapter 5.

4

Subject and Object Fused

The separation of the person as subject from the person as object persisted throughout the last two thousand years of intellectual history. As late as the first half of the twentieth century, psychologists were still concerned about the subjective nature of consciousness and whether it would be better to eliminate it as a concept from their lexicon.

There has always been a pendulum swing of psychological theories between those with subjective and those with objective emphases throughout recorded history. Even in cases where an attempt was made to eliminate the dichotomy it was usually accomplished by simply denying the validity of one or the other. In twentieth century American psychology subjective qualities presumably residing in consciousness were eliminated in favor of an objective behavioral analysis. Similarly, subjective theorists such as Freud (in some aspects of his theory) or Merleau-Ponty relegated objective analysis to a relatively unimportant position compared with description of subjective states. Virtually all theorists were uncomfortable with any tendency to account for both subjective and objective aspects of existence within the same theoretical framework.

However, as we shall see, there is at least one theory (Piaget's) that attempted to account for subjective and objective aspects of existence within the same set of theoretical principles and that kept subject and object epistemologically separate. Before we discuss attempts to fuse subject and object, we need first raise the question as to why theorists alternated between subject and object in their explanations.

In the Western world the Hume–Kant controversy set the intellectual motif for man's attempt to explain himself. The Western mind seemed to leap quickly to the idea that one is either an emanation or effect of a string of causal sequences begun from outside, or that the world consists of emanations from self. The fact that there has been a constant shift between theories that can be identified as objective or subjective indicates that there is a fundamental difficulty with taking either one of these positions consistently. The limits of the truth or usefulness of one position are both revealed and adjusted by the other. But what has constantly escaped theorists is the possibility of logically and empirically fusing the two positions so that a single coherent interpretation emerges. We have seen that if one makes the assumption that an understanding of human existence is yielded from a study of sense data, the resulting theory will be concerned with object. This position will forever exclude aspects of human existence, such as thought, that cannot be derived from sense data.

Similarly, a subjective position based on some form of self-awareness, where the individual acts as center, motivator, and concluder, is forever estranged from the possibility that much apparently complex data may be determined by a series of simple reactive links with external stimuli. In short, the individual under certain circumstances might very well act in an objectlike way.

We saw in the previous chapter that the phenomenologists attempted to fuse subject and object. However even this attempt, in the eyes of an objectivist, is seen as subjective. We have also seen that the phenomenological position includes the idea that the individual's processes are not separable from things thought about, that touching is not separable from things touched. The separation of these is, of course, the classic distinction between subject and object. In that sense, the phenomenologists have succeeded at least in defining the problem differently from their subjective and objective theoretical predecessors.

At this juncture let it suffice to indicate that definitional clarity and conceptual resolution of the subject–object problem is a part of the fusion that the phenomenologists accomplished. However, they lacked a procedure that yields the satisfaction of either the scientific method or the thoroughgoing subjectivism of a Kant or a Hegel. The phenomenological method is essentially careful description of immediate experience. But description, however satisfying in terms of a felt recognition of an aspect of existence, yields no causal line and therefore no possible prediction that is definite and examinable. There is, for all human beings, a certain satisfaction in the ability to predict specifically an event, but this requires a causal type of interpretation. Phenomenology has, I believe, adequately demonstrated that certain aspects of human existence are not amenable to causal analysis so that description is all that is available in these cases. Subjectivists have few terms to deal with the nature of a reflex, whereas objectivists have really nothing to say about the nature of logic. A subjective description may be examined against one's life experiences but not tested in any of the scientific ways in which Anglo-American thinkers are comfortable.

Quite often psychologists, particularly Americans, have cited the success of science in physics, biology, and chemistry as an argument for applying the scientific method to the study of human beings. The assumption is that the data that are relevant to the understanding of human beings are epistemologically the same as the data relevant to the understanding of the entities of physics, chemistry, and biology. I suggest that most of the epistemological character of the data of psychology is not the same as that of physics, chemistry, and biology. The part that is the same usually overlaps the subject matter of biology; for example, biochemical elements that influence behavior need to be understood in the terms of biology and chemistry. However, those aspects of human activity in which most people are interested seem to be epistemologically different from the subject matter of physics, chemistry, or biology.

Sigmund Koch (1956), made the point 20 years ago that it is necessary to consult the phenomena of human experience as well as human behavior. Indeed, he argued that it is necessary to develop theories of our own activities as scientists or as human beings. He was particularly concerned about the use of motivational variables to supply reasons for human behavior. His point was that much human behavior is intrinsically motivated or rather is intrinsically performed for reasons that have nothing to do with causal sequences extrinsic to the organism.

The unique character of much psychological data requires unique methods and theoretical concepts. Consequently, it is not possible to do a classical experiment and understand significant portions of certain psychological data. For example, there are elements of cognitive behavior that are simply not amenable to experiment, not because the conceptual and mechanical tools have not been developed, but because they are not epistemologically amenable to the logic of an experiment. This does not imply that the lack of a possibility for applying experiment to the solution of a given problem in psychology eliminates rationality and reason. In all cases, nonexperimental analysis needs to be both consistent with empirical facts and logically cohesive.

An empirical logical analysis of a generative grammar is a case in point. A good deal of information has been gathered from a rational nonexperimental analysis of a grammar of language (Chomsky, 1964, 1966). (We shall discuss this below.) There is a controversy attached to this effort in that there are those who believe it is possible to understand and even produce a language by experimental means, that is, via conditioning (for example, Skinner, 1957). The argument against the acquisition of language structures via conditioning is tied to the nature of what it means to make an inference and therefore also to the idea of causality. The process of inference making is never solely reducible to the juxtaposition of objects or processes involved in such an inference, but always reflects a basic inferential characteristic of the inferer. This position is discussed in some detail in *Assumptions of Social Psychology* (Lana, 1969a).

What can be said if there are inadequacies in all objective and subjective positions and in phenomenology concerning the fusion of subject and object? I would propose at this point that although I believe human beings are best described in their daily lives by the phenomenological approach, there will always be an epistemological necessity for separating object from subject. The reason is that although man is ultimately not separable from the objects of his thought or perception, he can and does see himself or parts of himself as objectlike and other parts as subjectlike. In Chapter 10 we will discuss in some detail how, and under what circumstances, humans see themselves as objects or as under the influence of others who perceive them as objects. This problem is related to the general ethical context of psychology.

There can be a conscious movement away from a sense of existence or phenomenological context into perceiving oneself as object in a variety of epistemologically important situations. In a sense this is what makes so many reasonably well-thought-out and somewhat empirically verifiable psychological systems equivalent in terms of one's choice among them. They all have a certain degree of correctness because humans can be many things. This implies that in certain areas of human existence, which we shall enumerate in ensuing chapters, objective scientific method is not the only useable approach to solving problems. In some instances there are logical impossibilities; in others the empirical problems are so great as to render an objective approach useless. Socio-political problems and certain problems in cognition may not be amenable to scientific technique. In these cases, something like phenomenological analysis may be more appropriate. There are other areas where a scientific, objective method is successful, for example, areas involving physiological processes.

Perhaps the clearest example of the supplementary quality of phenomenal and scientific descriptions of ostensibly the same phenomenon can be made with regard to the physiology and phenomenal character of thought and language. Scientists have made concrete progress in understanding the seats in the brain of hearing and memory. That damage to the temporal lobes affects hearing is well established and indicates that that portion of the brain mediates this activity. Similarly, damage to the cortex selectively affects memory, depending on whether it was a recent or a more distant acquisition.

By and large classical study of brain physiology has localized certain functions such as hearing and memory to an extent that is extremely helpful in understanding the process whereby these functions, short circuited by cortical damage or surgical intervention, are enhanced or debilitated. There have even been theories of physiological brain cell change accompanying acquisition of language or use of speech (for example, Hebb, 1949). No physiological research on the central nervous system associated with speech, memory, or thinking in general has ever been complete. One may argue, as we have in other places in this book, that they cannot be completed so as to include all of the functional properties of speech, thinking, and memory. At the same time, there have been theories of thought and language usage (Chomsky, 1964, 1966; Skinner, 1957) that supplement these physiological theories but are essentially different in their composition. A case in point is the emphasis made by Noam

Chomsky with regard to his system of language acquisition and use. Language seems primarily a means of thought and self-expression. The self-expression is directed *to* one's self. This function supercedes the animal-like communication system that has been suggested by B. F. Skinner.

Normal human language is free from the control of independently identifiable external stimuli or internal physiological states. It is not restricted to any practical communicative function as occurs in simpler animals. Of central importance is the idea that grammatical structure, common to all languages, reflects certain fundamental similarities in thought among all human beings. Language universals set limits to the character of the vast variety of human languages. The fact that there are universal characteristics to languages suggests that people learn and think in the same way independently of their particular life experiences.

Descriptive linguistics, coupled with our knowledge of the physiological underpinnings of speech, memory, and active thought, yield our most comprehensive picture of the nature of thought. Although these two sets of information are supplemental, they remain epistemologically independent of one another. The physiological information is based on an accumulation of scientific data based on experiment. The analysis of thought and grammatical structure is based on a nonexperimental, empirical observation of the way language is used and a logical analysis of it.

A somewhat parallel situation exists regarding one of the classic problems of social psychology, namely, the formation of attitudes and the possibility of manipulating them in order to gain certain socially desirable results. Attitudes are developed in an individual over time as a process of learning. One of the key factors in this learning is generalization. That is, through either direct or indirect experience via cognitive review, an individual builds a set of emotionally charged predispositions to act or to believe certain things about a class of identifiable stimuli such as an ethnic group. Repeated negative experiences with members of this stimulus class, for example, Polish people, could produce negative responses via generalization on the part of the individual encountering not only specific Poles but any Pole. In short, it is believed that attitudes are developed via a process of conditioning and generalization.

Let us assume that a group of individuals has, over the years, developed a strong negative attitude toward another ethnic group via this process of conditioning and generalization. From other information about the conditioning process we know that it is possible to decondition individuals by substituting various reinforcements such that previously negative stimuli can take on neutral or positive charges.

If we are interested in the social engineering problem of eliminating prejudice in members of one group toward another, we first need to have them exposed to the proper learning situation. Indeed, much public money has been spent on trying to do just that. There are still compaigns attempting to convince people that they should not feel negative toward members of various ethnic groups. By and large, this attempt is, and must be, ineffective if it focuses solely on relearning. Although we know how to teach someone no longer to be prejudiced toward an individual, the immediate phenomena of his life or of his group's life create a situation where there may be a *vested interest* in maintaining a certain prejudice. Being prejudiced pays off in many ways as well as creating problems in an individual's or group's life. An aggressive pose may eliminate an alien group from competition for jobs or for low-cost housing. Consequently, simple learning must be considered within a sociological, historical, and political context.

Attitudes may not be changeable other than through their own natural rhythms. Because socio-political and economic phenomena often change rapidly, only a phenomenological description of attitude may be possible in such a situation. Should this be the case, it must be combined with the more deliberate scientific approach in order to maximize the probability of changing attitudes. Indeed, it is this phenomenological quality that quite often disallows any effective problematic change in social structure, policy, or action. Major social change by government-sponsored programs, short of direct coercion, may indeed be impossible since complex social situations arise and change dynamically by principles that may be better observed phenomenally than interfered with scientifically.

THE PHENOMENOLOGICAL ATTEMPT TO FUSE SUBJECT AND OBJECT

The ancient idea of association can be described as the tendency for a repeatedly occurring linkage of two ideas or events to create the situation where the appearance of one increases the probability of the memory of the other. We have seen that during the eighteenth century, laws of association such as similarity, cause and effect, and contiguity, were written. The general notion was that the ideas themselves could be accidently linked. In short, there needed to be no intrinsic meaning to the linkage of two ideas such that one would call up the memory of the other, but rather the simple juxtaposition or contiguity and similarity of the two ideas produced a dynamic connection.

Merleau-Ponty interpreted this process of association differently from either the eighteenth century associationists or their modern American counterparts such as Thorndike, Hull, and Skinner. Human beings have the ability, which they immediately comprehend, to intend their cogitations; that is, we have the ability to translate exactly from the objects we perceive in the world to our thought, which is identical to them. We immediately have objects in space perceptually in our thought. We see a table, which immediately registers smoothness, roundness, and so forth. If nearby there is an orange chair with a rough texture, this is also immediately perceived. Association is thus nothing more than the passive buildup of a bit of the world coming into us. Relational ability is immediately given to us. There is no need for a principle of association to account for the presence of a thought calling up the memory of another. Since there is no need for a principle of association for perception, there is also no need to invoke such a doctrine for ideas.

Merleau-Ponty did not deny the phenomenon of association but concluded that the doctrine of association is not necessary. The principle was needed in the first place because associationists saw the organism as a passive receiver of stimuli. Hence, the dynamic in the system had to be provided by some principle of action. Since the phenomenological point of view understands the organism to be active in that perception and ideas are immediately given, there is no need for a special principle of association.

Merleau-Ponty criticized the American notion that the acquisition of habit takes place by an association of stimulus with response and that this linkage itself is a principle of activity. He argued that a child who has previously burned himself will not repeat the sudden withdrawal of his hand in the presence of a flame. This, he said, indicates that there is not simply a correlation between the burning sensation and the hand movement, but rather that a conditioned stimulus is representative of an entire category of stimuli that have become reflexogenic. The original movement is established only as a particular instance of a general aptitude that can vary around the same theme. In short, the true stimulus is not the one defined by physics or chemistry, and therefore the response is not a particular series of movements. Rather, there is a characteristic of the organism that ensures that the learning experience will have a general relevance. Gestalt psychologists have often argued that the idea of learning as a succession of movements in a trial-and-error fashion was a product of the kinds of learning situations in which associationist psychologists placed animals. For example, in the Thorndike experiment when escape from a cage was made dependent upon manipulation of the lock, there was a tendency for the animal to respond in a steplike fashion.

The structure of understanding of human beings takes a dialectical as opposed to a mechanical form. Mechanical action is seen as the decomposability into concrete elements of cause and effect. The concrete elements have a one-to-one correspondence. In very simple actions, this dependence is unidirectional. The cause is the necessary and sufficient condition for the effect. The dialectical relationship supposes that physical stimuli act upon the organism only by eliciting a global response, which will vary qualitatively when the stimuli vary quantitatively (that is, no quantitative change is discernible in the response in relation to quantitative change in the stimuli). These stimuli play the role of occasions for the organism rather than of causes. Organismic reaction thus depends on the vital significance of the stimulus rather than on the material properties. Hence, this dialectical notion supposes meaning existing among stimulus elements and bodily reaction. Thus, intrinsic meaning suggests the possibility of an operative dialectic and hence a fusion that is always present among stimuli and organismic reaction.

From this, consciousness is defined (Merleau-Ponty, 1963) by "the possession of an object of thought or by transparence to itself; action is defined by a series of events external to each other" [p. 164]. All of these thoughts or events are juxtaposed but are not linked in any manner. Consciousness thus reenters psychology via the modern phenomenologists. However, consciousness is not defined by knowledge of self but rather goes beyond explicit knowledge. The structures of action and knowledge in which consciousness is engaged must thus be described.

Once one has reached the dialectic of subject and object, the body is no longer the cause of the structure of consciousness; rather, it has become its object. An old-fashioned psychophysiological parallelism is irrelevant since fusion has been accomplished.

Thus, phenomenal consciousness understands the dialectic that exists between self and world. It does not choose between subject and object the way experimental science has in the twentieth century. Rather, it eliminates both as viable concepts.

LANGUAGE AND PHENOMENAL EXPLANATIONS

Chomsky's (1964, 1966) theory of generative grammar is pertinent to the contrast we have made throughout this work between causative experimental and descriptive approaches to understanding human existence. A grammar attempts to describe and account for the ability of an individual to understand a sentence of his language, which he may not have heard before, and to produce a related sentence, which he may never have spoken. This competence can be described as a system of rules that relate verbal signals to an interpretation of the meaning of these signals. The most important characteristic of linguistic competence is the ability of the speaker to produce new sentences that are immediately understood by others. Chomsky denies the possibility of habit generaliations in accounting for the ability to construct these new sentences based on their similarity to old ones. He believes that the chronological evolution of linguistic possibilities in a child indicates that physiological development is more important than habit in producing language.

A syntactic description of a sentence can convey information beyond its phonetic form and semantic content. That portion is defined as the deep structure of a sentence. The surface structure of a sentence is that portion of the syntactic description that determines its phonetic form. There are other elements to the system, but our purpose here is to focus upon certain key ideas that indicate the epistemological quality of this theory of generative grammar.

In order to uncover the deep structure of a nonambiguous sentence (ambiguous sentences have more than one deep structure) it is necessary to analyze the sentence into its components. Chomsky gives the following example: Consider the following sentence.

(1) I expected the man who quit work to be fired.

This sentence can be transformed into three kernal sentences.

(2) a.   I expected it
    b.   someone fired the man
    c.   the man quit work

In order to form Sentence (1) the three base structures underlying sentences (2a), (2b), and (2c) are dealt with as follows: Sentence (2c) is transformed so that it converts to "wh (the man) quit work." This new structure we label K_1. The "wh" represents a generalized morpheme that would appear in any sentence of the type 1 regardless of language. Hence, the letter designation of "who" is arbitrary. In the case of this English example, the "wh" that is approprite is "who." In other sentences containing the same morpheme, "which" or "what" might have been appropriate. By considering this new structure K_1 with Sentence (2b) and deleting the occurrence of the man in K_1 we get "someone fired the man who quit work," which we label K_2. We transform K_2 into a passive form, which yields, "the man who quit work was fired by someone," and label it K_3. A deletion transformation is applied to K_3, which yields, "the man who quit work was fired," which we label K_4. We combine (2a) and K_4 yielding, "I expected the man who quit work was fired," which we label K_5. To K_5 we apply a transformation T, which refers to the infinitive that was found in the original sentence.

This completes the analysis. By such techniques as the application of transformations of the sort suggested here, Chomsky presumably describes the deep structure of all languages since the concentration of the analysis is on its morphemological basis. Clearly, the kinds of transformations that are needed to isolate the useful qualities of a language are specifiable without exception and constitute a highly useful description of the way people think. This in turn implies, as Chomsky has suggested, that explanation of the acquisition of the normal use of language cannot be explained by concepts such as habit or learning or any other functional variable alone. The suggestion is that these deep structures are yielded mainly by the innate equipment of human beings such that thought may very well give shape and form to language rather than the other way around. Chomsky and others have already succeeded in describing language in a useful manner without recourse to experiment or contingent variables. This is not to imply that experiments cannot be generated from this analysis. However, they are a by-product of syntactical description.

One of the useful characteristics of language that is central to this approach is that it is dependent on structure for its meaning. Chomsky gives the following example: We can form a question out of a declarative sentence by a simple operation. We first identify a subject noun phrase of the sentence and move the occurrence of ''is'' following this phrase to the beginning of the sentence. The sentence, ''The dog in the corner is hungry'' contains the noun phrase, ''The dog in the corner.'' Moving the ''is'' that follows this to the beginning of the sentence, we form the question, ''Is the dog in the corner hungry?'' This is a structure-dependent operation since the operation considers not only the sequence of elements that form the sentence but also their structure. That is, the fact that ''The dog in the corner'' is a noun phrase indicates that the rule of this formation is dependent on this structure. A parallel ''structure-independent'' operation on the same sentence will not work. For example, the rule may be, ''take the left most occurrence of is and move it to the front of the sentence.'' This would yield by the structure-independent operation the question, ''Is the dog that in the corner is hungry?'' Clearly, this is incorrect. In applying the structure-dependent operation, we locate the noun phrase, ''the dog is in the corner,'' then invert the occurrence of ''is'' that follows it, forming the sentence, ''Is the dog that is in the corner hungry?''

Through this example, we can see that, although there is no differential communicative efficiency or simplicity between two sets of operations, there is a difference in duplicating the way people really use language in the structure-dependent operation. Indeed, Chomsky points out that if we were attempting to design a language via computer, we would prefer the structure-independent rule. Yet the formation of sentences proceeds without the simplicity of a computer and this fact illustrates the language-determining properties of thought. We shall see in the chapter on developmental psychology that the idea of a basic structure central to the nature of human understanding is also central to the work of Jean Piaget.

There is indirect but definite biochemical support for Chomsky's structural position with regard to the nature of human language. The evidence is indirect because Chomsky's analysis is descriptive of existing language usage while the discoveries in biochemistry concerning basic nucleic structures are more classically in the scientific experimental mode. Since this point is sufficiently important not only for our description of the nature of language and of the fusion of ideas of subject and object, but for basic epistemological considerations involving determinism and freedom, we will describe invariant enzyme structures following the presentation of Jacques Monod (1971).

MONOD'S CHANCE AND NECESSITY

The idea that living beings are endowed with a purpose or a project and that the keys to this purpose are found in their physical structure has often been rejected by biologists and biochemists. However, purpose is evident in performance.

The distinction between a living organism and an artifact lies principally in the easily observable fact that artifacts have been formed by forces exterior to the object itself while living material gains its structural properties, such as molecules and atoms, from its interior constitution. The internal deterministic code of a living organism is totally free of influence from outside factors determining its structure or performance.

Internal determining characteristics of living beings, at base, are invariant. This invariance determines their teleonomic nature and not the other way around, as much philosophical and religious thinking would have it. Monod believes that the teleonomic nature of living beings can be established in an objective scientific manner and that, therefore, the contradistinction between science and teleonomy is false. The specific hypothesis is that the evolution and refinement of teleonomic structures in the molecules of an organism are determined by changes occurring in a structure that already is endowed with the property of invariance. Teleonomy thus becomes a property of invariance in the genetic code. The basic organic invariant is DNA.

This quality of invariance is not only consistent with the selected theory of evolution but, indeed, supports it. The DNA molecule conveys information in designing a sequence of amino acids such that the structure and performance of resulting protein cannot be modified, nor is there any possibility for reverse information transition from protein to DNA. If there is no mechanism whereby any information can be transferred to DNA thereby modifying it, basic living structure is set within the nature of the DNA molecule. It is impervious to any influence from the outside world. Hence, there is no "dialectical" possibility existing within this molecular biological level. Among other things, this accounts for the fact that there is enormous stability among certain species that have reproduced for hundreds of millions of years without change, even though it is true that the DNA molecule can undergo perturbations that will slowly accumulate after eons of time.

Hence, given the necessity of the nature of basic biological structure, because of the invariance of the DNA molecule, chance or accidental occurrences in this structure are the only factors that bring about change. According to Monod, there is no possibility that the concept of this combination of chance and necessity (and, therefore, of the nature of basic living matter) will ever be changed. Monod concludes that language is the evolutionary end product that most characterizes the difference between human beings and other species. He accepts, apparently whole-heartedly, Chomsky's point that the underlying structure of all human languages is innate and characteristic of the species. This is consistent with the biological nature of the DNA molecule and with the implication that evolutionary sequence, including language, is determined, of necessity, by an internal factor rather than by acquisition from the outside. Both Monod and Chomsky appreciate the Cartesian dichotomous quality of this conclusion as opposed to the Hegelian notion of the dialectic.

Assuming that Monod's conclusions concerning the nature of DNA are justified, and evidence suggests this, the implications are enormous for basic epistemological issues attending modern psychology. Monod has suggested that an implication of this invariant quality of basic biological material champions even further the objective method of science at the expense of ''subjective methods'' typically found in philosophy and some psychology. He believes that consciousness is one of the few remaining areas where objective scientific method has not made an inroad but will in the future, thereby discrediting extant subjective methods and conclusions. However, the very cast of Monod's analysis, accepting as it does Chomsky's conclusions about the nature of language, throws doubt on the consistency of his epistemological position. Hence, in his general attack on subjectivism, he repudiates holistic approaches to the solution of human problems and creates the straw man of suggesting that holism in any form depreciates analysis. The best holistic approaches have never argued against the usefulness of objective analysis but rather have argued for the necessity to maintain functioning units at the level at which they actually operate in life. It may be pointed out that the principle of interaction found in statistics, a highly objective mathematical technique, is also a ''holistic'' principle.

Monod does not realize that the epistemological context of Chomsky's generative grammar is an analysis of meaning that begins with description of existing modes of speech. The power of the system is generated by its nonexperimental nonanalytical approach and its emphasis on a description of language as it exists in toto. It has attempted to preserve the holistic character of language. The fact that Chomsky concludes that the basic form of language is innate (and this is consistent with the immutable characteristics of the DNA molecule) both emphasizes the structural property of language and indicates that a ''holistic'' subjective epistemology that is imaginatively and carefully performed can yield information that is consistent with an objective experimental epistemology. Subjective method in its best form is careful description of evidence as it exists whereas the best form of the objective method is the experiment.

Even with these limitations, Monod's position is very important. One may summarize his major point by saying that research on the nature of the DNA molecule indicates that biological evolution rests upon mechanical, molecular invariance and this in turn implies that evolution is not a property of living organisms but rather is a property of a nonchanging mechanism. Evolution itself stems from inperfections in this mechanism. Monod takes this as a defense of objectivism in science. Yet in another argument he suggests that these very facts support Cartesian and Kantian subjectivism.

Monod has stated that there should be no differentiation between the operation of brain and mind and that this differentiation is an illusion. Yet, I would argue that the differentiation is no more illusory than Monod's choice of a Chomskian linguistic analysis over that of Skinner's, which is certainly more in the objective tradition. The point is that, epistemologically, the immutable determinism of the DNA molecule does not in any way affect the validity of the point that analysis of certain human phenomena needs to be holistic and descriptive rather than analytic and experimental. Regardless of the undoubted connection between the nature of the DNA molecule and physiological predispositions to language and thought, the epistemological characteristics of a Chomskian analysis that Monod accepts is closer to that of phenomenal description than to objective analysis.

Monod's rejection of the dialectic[1] suggests an interesting problem that follows from difficulties in Monod's analysis already suggested. He indicates, quite justifiably, the absurb application of the dialectic, particularly in the materialistic form, to biochemistry and evolution. Clearly, the influence of the structure of the DNA molecule disallows a biological evolutionary dialectic since the properties and influence schemes of that molecule are unchangeable and irreversible. However, the dialectic at the human behavioral or cognitive level may be valid. Human beings with their capacity for language may be understood in terms of a dialectic interplay among the cognitive, emotional, and motivational characteristics of their lives. A dialectic form is apparent in certain personality theories as we shall see in Chapter 6 as well as in social theories discussed in Chapter 7. In Chapter 8 we shall see that Piaget opposes Monod by suggesting that there is a dialectical structural basis to human cognitive functioning despite the immutable physiological development determined by the DNA molecule.

[1]The dialectic at the functional level can be illustrated within the context of Freudian theory. A child is confronted with a mother or a mother surrogate who is both a source of nurturance and therefore an object of love, and a source of pain via the rejection of direct gratification of nurturance because of the application of rules of delay that society requires. From the opposed tendencies can emerge an adult with a view of the world that includes the necessity of pleasure and pain as intrinsic parts of life. This view can be integrative and highly desirable both from clinical and societal notions of reality. What the child takes to be apparently paradoxical qualities in life are seen as fused in a meaningful way by the adult (see Chapter 6 for a more extensive discussion). In short, an adult synthesis of childhood antitheses can emerge.

5

The Nature of Data

The crucial manifestation of the epistemological positions already discussed is the datum that is central to each. Datum, in turn, is inseparable from the method that produces it. In examining the nature of data in the objective experimental, objective nonexperimental, logical, and phenomenological methods the possibilities for subject and object-oriented epistemological derivations will be drawn more closely.

EXPERIMENTAL DATA

A scientific experiment, in many ways, is a remarkably simple event, yet it sustains a power and elegance apparently out of proportion to this simplicity. The idea of an experiment is to recreate a part of the world in a controlled manner. A control implies that an experimenter is able to manipulate key aspects of the experimental situation. The degree that these manipulations are quantifiable is the degree to which the experiment is precise. Difficulties with the applicability or meaning of experiments depend upon the bit of the world that the experimenter has chosen to examine under these controlled conditions. If it is trivial or it is irrelevant to his purpose, the experiment to that extent is useless or less useful than it would be were he able to recreate a significant or meaningful bit of the world in a controlled situation. It is usually the case that the more precision the experimenter can maintain in the experimental situation, the less important the problem he is studying. Conversely, the more important the bit of the world he brings into the experimental situation, the less able he is to control precisely the elements of the experiment. This is particularly the case when human beings are his subjects.

Since the problems that people consider important within the framework of their own lives are those that have to do with other people, there are a large number of operant variables that increase the difficulty of control. Also, the human subject maintains his humanity in an experiment. He perceives how *he* is perceived by others within the framework of the study. In short, he knows he is in an experiment. This makes the individual's phenomenal world, as described in Chapter 3, relevant to the meaning of an experiment but not necessary to its method. As we have seen, the phenomenal world is not amenable to experimental manipulation or control without directly changing its experiential character. Experiment is not applicable when a problem involves an individual's sense of his place in the world. If it is desirable for an individual to learn how to do something quickly and efficiently (for example, drive a car) experimental research on that subject will be very helpful. What the individual learns may be a bit of important information for him, yet it may not touch his sense of self. If it does (for example, I am now more manly because I can drive a car), it does so because he has interpreted the learned act within a sociopersonal context that places a value on it. However, this fact is not contained as a variable within the manipulations used to teach him to drive.

THE SIMPLE STRUCTURE OF AN EXPERIMENT

An experiment has one or more independent variables, which are those events quantitatively manipulated by the experimenter. The dependent variable is the object or event that is presumably influenced by the manipulation of the independent variables. It is the event in which the experimenter is principally interested. The extent that the experimenter is able to quantitatively control the independent variables in a precise manner is the extent to which their effect on the dependent variable will be most precisely measured. However, the relevance of the independent and dependent variables to the knowledge that the experimenter wishes to gain is problematic and not contained as a possibility within the framework of the experiment. It is more influenced by the imagination and ingenuity of the experimenter. Control is accomplished by applying rules of logic to the conclusion drawing that is made about the results of the experiment.

THE SUBJECT OF AN EXPERIMENT

However the subject of an experiment reacts to the manipulations of the experimenter, he may have reacted that way for a variety of reasons. This fact establishes the necessity for control in any given experimental situation. Let us assume that the independent variable has affected the dependent variable. There is still the problem that a human subject, being in an experimental situation, responds differently from the way he would have in an appropriate real-life situation. Aside from these problems, which most experimenters understand, there is another that is not always acknowledged.

It is clear that in the experimental situation the subject himself becomes part of the structure of the experiment and, as an event, has roughly equal empirical status to the independent and dependent variables. Also, if the dependent and independent variables are treated as objects and are quantified, phenomenal existence, as we have described it above, can play no part in an experiment.

THE STRUCTURE OF CONTROL

Since all psychological experiments are designed to test an hypothesis of change from an initial state of the organism to some other state as a result of an experimental treatment, the relevant state of the organism must be initially determined. Either initial states of an organism can be measured and differences in that state assessed after the application of experimental treatment, or the state of the organism can be created by some manipulation of the experimenter prior to the experimental treatment, thus eliminating the need for a measure of the pretreatment state (Lana, 1969b).

The ideal experiment is one in which the relevant preexperimental state of the organism is determined without affecting that state by the very measuring process itself. Unfortunately, it is rarely possible to achieve this since it is almost always necessary to manipulate the environment of the subject in some way in order to determine its preexperimental state. It is, as I have mentioned, this preexperimental treatment that may very well influence the subject to respond differently than he would have, had he not been involved in this prior manipulation.

A case in point is that involving the measurement of a change in social attitude as a result of a persuasive communication. In order to determine the effectiveness of a persuasive argument to convince people of a certain social or political point of view, it is necessary to first determine the attitude of the individual toward that subject matter. In order to determine this initial attitude, the individual must be exposed to a measuring device of some sort. If he is, it may set him in some way to suspect that he is in an experimental situation, and hence any succeeding communication might interact with this perception and yield a different result, had he not been premeasured.

In short, knowing that one's attitude is being measured might affect the way one receives a communication that is clearly designed to change it. Although some of these interactive effects can be minimized, the basic problem remains of the experimenter interfering with what he wants to know about the subject. This interference increases with the perceived importance of the problem. Since important problems are often experiential in nature, the applicability of the experiment to understanding the human social condition may indeed be minimal.

EXPERIMENT AND THERAPY

Within the past several years, techniques have been developed that apply the simple principles of an experiment to psychological therapy. The intent of the application is to produce desirable behavioral change in the patient. The similarity between an experiment and this type of therapy is that an independent variable is imposed upon the patient with the expectation that a certain type of response will follow. The response may be conceived of as the dependent variable. The goal is to link an input by the therapist with an output by the patient. This linkage, although it may be of great practical importance, can by itself yield no explanation as to why the patient responds as he does and why he changes. If behavior modification is achieved, the therapist may see no need to delve into the reasons for his success, and an implicit assumption may grow (as indeed it has) that the human organism is an object in its essential properties and thus can be dealt with and understood in all that that implies.

McGuire and Vallance (1964) applied a behavior modification technique to a 29-year-old teacher who was initially disturbed by obsessional thoughts about his wife's fidelity. These thoughts apparently began as a result of a remark about his wife made by his mother. Since the mother's statement was sufficiently ambiguous, he realized that his obsessions had no basis in reality. Nevertheless, he could not control these disturbing ideas. The modification technique that was applied was based on the idea that as a response such as the obsessional thought is immediately paired with a noxious stimulus such as an electric shock, there will be a tendency on each successive occasion for the frequency and the strength of the obsession to be diminished. This prediction is consistent with our general knowledge of the nature of aversive conditioning. The therapeutic treatment that McGuire and Vallance applied to this patient consisted of electric shocks being contiguously applied with the subject's thoughts about his mother's making the remark about his wife or with thoughts about the implications of that remark. After the initial session with the patient, he himself controlled the timing and intensity of shock administration. After this, he continued this conditioning process at home with a portable shock apparatus. The authors reported that within a relatively short period of time his obsessions were eliminated and he was generally less anxious.

Clearly, the form of the therapy is consistent with the form of any number of classic experiments done in aversive conditioning. The implicit assumption is that the organism will respond to a stimulus (the shock), which has no intrinsic relationship to the obsessional thoughts but does have a certain power in influencing the individual because it produces pain. There seems to be no question that the purpose of eliminating the obsession was achieved, but the question of why this happened remains unanswered. Researchers in behavior modification typically do not concern themselves with theoretical interpretations of their work. They are usually concerned with the result of the therapy, which hopefully has some positive value to the subject. This is well and good, and certainly no one would argue that a technique that relieves pain and anxiety should not be used for such purpose if it has no negative side effects. However, as was suggested above, there is an implicit view of the nature of man held by any researcher who continuously utilizes this type of experiment. Indeed, there are a number of systems of explanation of human beings that are of this functional-contingency variety, such as the systems of B. F. Skinner (1953), Joseph Wolpe (1958), and others. An extended discussion of the nature of this type of system is provided in *Assumptions of Social Psychology* (Lana, 1969a).

The results of the McGuire and Vallance experiment can be interpreted in a number of ways, particularly with reference to why the self-punishment is successful in modifying behavior. Remember that, aside from the initial few trials of the study, the subject himself carried about a portable generator and self-administered shock when he experienced some manifestation of the obsession. The implication from McGuire and Vallance is that the desire to avoid shock was the determiner of the elimination of the obsession. However, it is clear that since the shock was self-administered, the patient could have eliminated the shock by simply not administering it to himself. Thus, some other element is operating besides the simple avoidance of the obsessional thought via the application of shock. It is also true that when the individual eventually ceased to use the shock apparatus, he should have also eventually ceased to repress the obsessional thoughts.

This was not the case in this study. That is, in any operant conditioning paradigm, when reinforcement is stopped the organism continues to respond up to a point and then eventually extinguishes. Various schedules of reinforcement, of course, can maintain the response for longer periods of time than others. In all cases, the removal of reinforcement should eventuate in extinction of the previous reinforced response. Thus, if a patient no longer responds the way he did as a result of this kind of therapy, some other process would have had to be operating other than the reinforcement contingency. One possibility is that the patient might have, with his willingness to go to the therapist and then to undergo this particular therapy, reexamined his life. A conclusion we may draw at this point is that a behavior modification technique of this type can be effective, but only under circumstances where the individual either prepares himself or is prepared by the therapist to accept such a treatment. This preparation implies some self-reconstruction of life possibilities. We will discuss this in further detail in Chapter 6 on modern personality theories.

We can further examine a reinforcement contingency as it is perceived and dealt with by its recipient in a manner that should make clear what is actually happening in an individual who is receiving the reinforcement. Let us assume that on successive punishing experiences the response that the individual wishes to eliminate actually does diminish until eventually it disappears, and this result lasts when the individual is out of the therapeutic situation and back in society. The assumption is that the behavior has indeed been modified and that this implies that reinforcement contingencies on successive trials involving the desired behavior and punishment are what actually account for the removal of symptoms.

The analysis may be carried further. The individual had to decide to submit himself to this sort of therapy in the first place. Although a behavior modification therapist can ignore this bit of behavior by concentrating upon the goal of eliminating a particular response, it cannot be ignored if we are to understand the total functioning of a particular individual. The point is that the patient chose to eliminate the particular behavior. He therefore made a choice to come to a therapist. Once discovering what the therapy was about, he had to choose to submit himself to it. This implies that the behavior was sufficiently undesirable so that the individual would make these often difficult choices. Even in the midst of the application of therapy, the individual could, of course, resist it, but he chose not to.

The degree to which the elimination of the behavior is automatic, that is, not under voluntary control of the individual, is not examined in modification situations since the individual's immediate motivation is mainly to eliminate the behavior. Therefore, we can say that his choice in the matter is consistent with what the therapist believes he should be doing. This indicates that the phase of the relationship between therapist and patient that establishes the acceptance by the patient of the techniques of the therapist is of singular importance. Perhaps the establishment of this relationship is of greater importance than the actual modification technique itself. This relationship occurs on a level considerably different from the exchanges inherent in a reinforcement modification experience and is subject to all the limitations and possibilities of phenomenological inquiry.

We know that it is also possible for an individual to rid himself of a given behavior, although it may be difficult, simply by inhibiting it in the appropriate situation by his own conscious choice. If one has a habit of smoking, as difficult as it may be to break it, it is possible to simply stop without first tapering off. We would attribute this success more to a cognitive, decisional variable than to an automatic behavior sequence. The point is that in no way does behavior modification exclude the existential context (or vice versa) or other contexts that may be more explicative of an individual's action. Rather than choice being nonexistent or being abdicated by the individual in the behavior modification situation, it may be extremely active and is simply not attended to by the therapist who utilizes this process. The question as to whether an existential psychotherapy works better than a behavior modification psychotherapy, is problematic and undoubtedly has a great deal to do with the particular individual involved as well as his cultural *milieu*. The final point we might make is that behavior modification is conceptually equivalent to the scientific experiment and is therefore subject to all its limitations and possibilities regarding application to human beings.

The experiment within psychological research tends to work best when those aspects of human existence that are of interest have objectlike quality, and works least well when the subjective core of existence generated from the interaction of a human being with his environment is under examination. Hence, experimentation in psychology involving the physiology and simple behavior patterns of organisms is more successful than experimentation involving the human being in his relationship with other people or in his concept of self.

As I pointed out elsewhere (Lana, 1969a) even in functional systems that attempt to explain human behavior, such as those proposed by B. F. Skinner, C. L. Hull, or others, it is necessary that the theoretician bring to the set of objective contingencies that relate stimuli and responses an understanding as to what these relationships mean in a larger context. An experiment establishes a function between independent (input) and dependent (output) variables, which are related quantitatively. Ideally, this function is written and presented as the results of several experiments. In the case of certain modern behavioral theories the explanation is nothing more than a presentation of several functions. These functions allow one to predict the dependent variable from the appearance of the independent variable(s). The theorist must already have a context given by his own phenomenal experience invoking possibilities for knowing, in order to accept a functional statement as a level of explanation in the first place. One either immediately understands a functional statement, as one does a syllogism, or conceptually refers it to a theoretical system. A similar point, made above, is that the subject of a behavior modification brings a conceptual and decisionary context to that situation.

In any of the derivations of general behaviorism, or in many of the other systems of modern psychology, explanation is never more than prediction. One can always legitimately question as to where the predicted functional contingencies are placed within a theoretical system. There is also the question as to how one comes to know the tenets of induction or deduction used within a scientific prediction of human behavior. Epistemological questions of this sort are always legitimate when directed at a theory purporting to explain a major portion of human existence. The answer to this question will undoubtedly indicate that the nature of induction and deduction is a phenomenon external to any derivable from the results of a scientific experiment. We shall pursue this issue in Chapter 8.

EXPERIMENTAL ARTIFACTS
IN STUDYING HUMAN BEINGS

One of the difficulties of doing psychological experiments with human beings as subjects has resulted in what have been called artifacts in experimental research (Rosenthal & Rosnow, 1969). One of the simplest ways to describe this problem is by pointing out that human beings are probably the only experimental subjects that know they are in an experiment. This, of course, is not true of planets, steel spheres, or, most probably, animals different from humans. It has long been suspected that awareness that an individual is in an experiment may alter the responses that one receives from him.

An analogue to these artifacts can be found within experimental physics where subatomic particles are measured. This attempt at measurement has yielded what have been called "uncertainty effects" or the Heisenberg principles. When an attempt is made to measure simultaneously the position and velocity of an electron, one or the other changes in the process of measurement. The act of using a photon of light with the electron to be examined will change its position or speed. There is no way to correct this mensurative interference through the use of more sophisticated methodology.

Within human research, the artifactual areas that have been under heaviest investigation are those of (1) the subject's suspiciousness of the intent of the experimenter, (2) the effects of using volunteers as subjects, (3) pretest sensitization, (4) demand characteristics of experiments, (5) experimenter expectancy effects, and (6) evaluation apprehension.

1. In most social psychological research, the experimenter deceives the subjects with regard to the topic of the research. With populations of college students and others used as subjects that grow more and more sophisticated, the subject eventually becomes suspicious of the intent of the experimenter when he is participating in an experiment. This, of course, can cause problems with the nature of the results.

2. Human subjects who volunteer for an experiment are quite often psychologically different than those who do not volunteer. Consequently, a whole body of literature has developed in examining the effects of volunteer subjects on the results of experiments.

3. Because the relevant state of the organism must be determined before an experimental treatment can be applied in a psychological experiment, it is necessary to assess this state in the organism before the experiment proper begins. If this is done by some sort of pretest examination, this pretest examination may sensitize the individual to the experimental treatment thus creating an artifactual situation. In the absence of an examination of preexisting conditions before experimentation, the experimenter may be plagued with not

knowing the baseline performance of the subject on the relevant dependent variable.

4. Opposite to the suspiciousness that the subject may feel toward the experimenter is, what may be a tendency in many subjects to want to cooperate with the experimenter and give him what they think he wants. Hence, one can speak of the demand characteristics of a study in that the subject quite often may try to assess what it is the experimenter wishes from him rather than responding to the independent variables in a way most natural for him. These demand characteristics have been examined particularly in the fields of hypnosis and in helping behavior.

5. The interaction between the experimenter and the subject particularly regarding likes and dislikes may also affect the results of an experiment.

6. In some situations, the subject is afraid of being evaluated, is tense in the experimental situation, and will not perform in a way that is similar to the way he would, were he not tense. In short, an evaluation apprehension is present.

The crucial question that one may raise with respect to these artifacts that arise with experimentation on human beings, is whether the methodologies are correctable so as to eliminate the artifacts or whether they are inherent, as the Heisenberg principles, in the process of *any* experimental measurement. The current process of experimentation and measurement with human beings may be in a sufficiently primitive state so that many of the gross artifacts can be eliminated and hence more valuable information gathered — even though the ultimate process of experimental measurement always involves an ultimate artifact. With regard to the measurement of subatomic particles, even though the uncertainty exists, it is possible for a physicist to measure the velocities and positions of a group of electrons, although it is not possible to determine velocity and position for any one. Hence, although experimental measurement is limited in this case, it still permits accumulation of a great deal of information. Likewise, there have been suggestions concerning experiments on human beings as to how to eliminate various artifacts. For example, there are a variety of ways to measure human responses indirectly so that the person is not aware of being measured.

The other possibility is that although certain obvious artifacts might be eliminated from experimental measurement with human beings, we may never be able to accumulate correct information about certain aspects of human existence that are very important to us, since the act of experimentation and the subject's awareness of it, however dim, may change his immediate experience so that the phenomenon being studied is thereby also changed. What one emphasizes is a matter of taste. Both possibilities, to attempt to eliminate artifacts as much as possible or to shift from experimental measurement to phenomenal analysis, may be equally good. However, it seems clear that classical experimentation is ultimately limited as an epistemology in explaining the nature of human beings.

NONEXPERIMENTAL EMPIRICAL DATA

It is both possible and necessary to observe individuals or animals in various situations without being able to control them. In many instances, control is not possible since the activity in which one is interested takes place in a rather broad context within the natural habitat of the organism. Ecological studies are of this sort. In many instances it is either impractical to recreate the natural habitat of the animal in the laboratory or impossible to duplicate complex natural conditions.

In clinical psychology observation is often possible without the experimenter being able to exercise experimental control over the client. The observations themselves may be used in many ways. It is, of course, possible to classify the observations into objective categories in much the same manner as one does the results of an experiment. In this case, the data are subject to the same limitations as any experimental investigation. However, since observations without attempts at experimental control are often made in the natural habitat of the organism, it is also possible for a broader picture to emerge. The observer may discover levels of meaning that are not directly observable but that are inferable from this broad context. Freudian psychoanalysis is of the type where these sorts of inferences are made. Conclusions, of course, are subject to further demonstration. Nonexperimental observation, however, suffers from a lack of precision, unlike experimental manipulation.

Konrad Lorenz (1966) studied a variety of species in their natural habitat, one of which was the three-spined male stickleback. It will attack any other male stickleback in a variety of situations but will avoid a similar attack on a female or on male members of other fish species. This bit of observation led Lorenz and others to hypothesize that a certain visual element of the male was the key stimulus for the attack. Through a series of experiments, it was determined that the red underbelly of the male was that stimulus. This was determined by introducing successively into the tank of the male stickleback a variety of models that contained one or more stickleback characteristics. By this method of successive experimental approximations, the red underbelly was determined to be the appropriate stimulus.

In this instance, the linkage between nonexperimental observation and experiment is apparent, the former acting as a heuristic device for the latter. A variety of personality theories were developed in a similar manner on the basis of nonexperimental observation. From these observations, the theorist, using his own logico-deductive talents, developed a set of ideas as to why people act as they do. In some instances experiments followed these leads (Dollard & Miller, 1950).

Thus, in many instances observation is propaedeutic to experimentation and is often used in conjunction with it. In other instances (for example, within the context of psychoanalysis), it is used as a description in order to make inferences that have no possibility of empirical experimental validation but that may convince the observer that they are true because of their logical and empirical coherence.

HISTORICAL METHOD

One of the prime methods of the nonexperimental empirical approach to developing knowledge about human beings is often used by historians, sociologists, and anthropologists. This method is the examination of documents and artifacts produced during a given period in the development of human beings. Psychology has typically not used this method. More traditional scientific and philosophical methods seem to lend themselves to the accumulation of psychological knowledge. Furthermore, historical techniques have never particularly been appreciated in psychology. We saw in Chapter 2 that Giambattista Vico, using historicoanthropological data in the late seventeenth and early eighteenth centuries, was able to provide not only information about the structure of language but hypotheses concerning the development of at least one major European civilization. One of the great difficulties with the examination of historical data has been that the validity of conclusions drawn from them has remained problematic.

If we look for a moment at the nature of historical data, certain characteristics immediately emerge. Because, by definition, we are dealing with events in the past, there is logically no possibility of applying an experimental method to verify a given conclusion, nor are the logical possibilities inherent within mathematics very useful. Predictions cannot be made that have very much usefulness because of the time dimensions involved and the complexities of historical information, even though some historians such as Arnold Toynbee (1962) have attempted to do just this. The historical method may be used as a heuristic device to develop ideas that might be used to gather empirical information, which may be amenable to more direct methods of validation. Vico succeeded in doing this in his theory of social origins. In essence, Vico invented the technique of utilizing philology in sociological analysis. He was able to do this because he was sensitive to historical perspective as a distinct technique in understanding civilization. Besides its heuristic quality, historical information provides a completeness to knowledge of the development of a civilization and, therefore, a completeness to an individual self inextricably involved in it.

From an epistemological point of view, the reconstruction of social origins and the examination of social progress and change needs to be made in two complementary ways: From philology, history, archaeology, and anthropology one can reconstruct the social activity and general character of the past in the manner of Vico. From knowledge of the psychology, biology, and sociology of modern people living in given societies, the remainder of the picture of modern man emerges. The latter disciplines possess methods best suited for problems dealing with individuals. The former are necessary to understand the historical scope of human beings and therefore are better used to comprehend, among other topics, ethics. The relationship between epistemology and ethics will be discussed in the final chapter of this volume.

When a sociopolitical analysis is made, the data on which it is based come from official documents (which presumably reflect the actual intent of politicians) and observation of contemporary social events. This information is then interpreted by a theorist. This latter phase of historical analysis is no different from its counterpart within the scientific experiment. The differences in the procedures between the two exist at the level of the initial data, which are input to the system. There is no repeatability of events in the case of historical analysis. Also, the events recorded are generally more complex than those controlled within an experiment. Hence, the accumulation of error is greater in the historical situation. However, the differences in this initial input quite often obscure the fact that both historical and scientific analysis depend upon the characteristics of the interpreter, both in terms of his observational and logical abilities and his unique life experiences and perspectives. In short, the theorist's own thought processes are intrinsic to the interpretation he makes. Theorists engaged in interpreting another person's position or actions are most susceptible to the possibility of error.

As we have seen above, within the context of both physics and psychology, prediction breaks down and theoretical conditions are radically altered at the frontiers of a discipline (that is, Heisenberg effects and artifacts in behavioral research). This may also be true for historical analysis. Technology and man's reactions to changes in it may not be predictable in their most important aspects because the conditions that would ordinarily allow prediction change radically.

For example, one of the classic predictions of Karl Marx (1936) is that, as a result of a struggle among various classes of a society, succeeding revolutions will occur, the ultimate and most important one being the one that terminates in the proletariat overthrowing the controlling middle class and assuming power over production, distribution of goods, and government in general. The major motivation for this final revolution is that the proletariat desires the fruits of its own labor and is driven to revolt on the basis of the inequitable distribution of goods then existing in a capitalist society. Although, clearly, the question is still open, what Marx did not foresee was that technological advances in the production and distribution of goods would be so rapid and so efficient that a large part of the proletariat would be inexorably pulled up into the middle class simply because there were so many goods to be distributed. Of course, this has happened in only a few countries of the world, but they have been politically important. That is, an economically dominating class within a society might be so successful in the production and distribution of goods among its own members that the technology it creates succeeds in allowing huge surpluses of goods, which then can be circulated to the underclasses profitably without damage to that controlling class. When this occurs, the distribution of goods among the proletariat exceeds everyone's wildest dreams and thoughts of revolution disappear.

Today, we see the strongest negative aspects of advancing technology; namely, the pollution of the environment and the using up of virtually every natural resource available to man. This development, of course, could lead to a scarcity of products in which case the old class struggles may reappear. If this does happen, the cycle would be much different from what Marx foresaw, since he was not fully appreciative of the insidious and profound influence of technology on the lives of people.

CONCLUSIONS

Historical analysis allows people to create and understand their own lives in continuity with the universe. Religion, with its implication of an afterlife, has also traditionally allowed for this continuity. Since very few modern theoreticians look to religion or an afterlife for either explanation or satisfaction, a sense of continuity must then come from history. An individual has always existed to himself even though he understands that he had a beginning and will have an end. This fact alone can create an immediate sense of meaninglessness when looked upon within the context of universal time spans. Relating oneself to one's ancestors and, indeed, to one's unborn generations allows some sense of continuity with the universe and thus creates a feeling of possibility for some individual meaning. This aesthetic cannot be minimized as part of the context for understanding human beings.

LOGIC AND MATHEMATICS

Within the context of virtually all experimentation and all nonexperimental observation, there is the use of mathematics and logic to make inferences about the data generated. In no way can these logico-mathematical structures be reduced to the actual observations made within the context of the experiment or of nonexperimental observation. This is, whatever one observes, the treatment of that data with regard to the inferences about it is a separate enterprise, which has more to do with the nature of the inferer than it does with the data being observed. This is treated in some detail in Chapter 2 of *Assumptions of Social Psychology* (Lana, 1969a) and our discussion to this point has included demonstrations as to why the separation between the nature of empirical data and inferences made about it is a logical one.

One of the ways man has of dealing with the world is through mathematics and logic. They are, in part, similar in nature to what Kant has called the categories of mind in that they are manifestations of the way man thinks. We shall discuss in a later chapter how mathematical structures can be part of both the genetics and experience of human beings when we discuss the ideas of Jean Piaget.

Mathematicians have built mathematical systems that have no apparent relationship to the empirical world. These systems contain their own internal rules of procedure. They have no empirical relevance. The sole requirment is that they be internally consistent. Often in the history of science, these man-created mathematical systems have been applicable to problems that have arisen within the empirical world. Since these systems were developed by mathematicians without reference to empirical observations, they could not have been directly given by the empirical conditions of the world of objects. Thus logic and mathematics are a third major data source, since understanding their generation in human beings is of central importance to epistemology.

PHENOMENOLOGICAL DATA

It was established in Chapter 3 that phenomenological data is immediate and is not subject to scientific or traditional philosophical analysis. The general method of phenomenology is description. This description must depict events as exactly as possible without analysis, comment, or value judgments of any sort. This is, of course, extremely difficult but not impossible. It is reflected in the ability of certain psychologists, novelists, and others to "capture" a situation that truly reflects one of life's important instances in description. This very emphasis on the description of existential states fuses psychology — particularly social and clinical—with the arts of fictional writing, film making, and, to a lesser degree, painting and sculpture.

The steps of a phenomenological description take the form of what have been called phenomenological reductions (Husserl, 1960, 1964; Merleau-Ponty, 1962, 1963). There are various levels at which one may describe the phenomenal event. The first phenomenological reduction makes its appearance from the moment we take the perceiving subject into account. That is, one may notice that a die is in front of him alone, perhaps the people nearby do not see it; it becomes the pole of a personal history, however minor an event it may be.

Secondly, one notices that the die is presented to him *only through sight*. This is the second reduction; thus one is left only with the outer surface of the die. It loses its materality and is reduced to a visual structure of form, color, light, and shade, but these are not in a void; they still retain a point of support that is the visual thing itself. This completes a set of reductions.

By a third reduction, we pass from the visual thing to the perspective aspect of the die. Through a final reduction one arrives at the sensation that is no longer a property of the thing but is a modification of one's body. The thing is both a correlative of a knowing body and reflects that body.

Perception of other people follows a similar course in a phenomenological interpretation. We are not in society as an object among objects, nor is society within ourselves as an object of thought. Society is felt in concrete terms as in any perceptual or reflective process.

An example of the phenomenal character of self and objective attributes assigned to it can be made if we think of an individual who is physically crippled in some way. The only way in which that individual can have a "cripple consciousness" is when he compares himself with others in a statistical and objective manner (very few people have a hunched back). Otherwise, he is simply an individual with a self that is independent of the objective facts that can be derived from it. One might note that this observation is the foundation of many existential psychotherapies. For example, it is held that the characteristics of typical neuroses as defined by objective categories are those characteristics that are superimposed on an individual by comparison with others. If the self is whole but is interfered with by these comparisons, then therapy becomes a "peeling away" of objective overlay in order to get to the existential self. That is, it is an attempt to allow the patient to realize the centrality and freedom of self—freedom to see objective entities as they really are: continuous with a central core of self.

HUMAN POTENTIAL

Phenomenology seeks to examine human beings in terms of their conditions of possibilty. By examining direct experience closely, one will see the possibilities for human existence. Noematic reflection originates in the reason of the subject itself. The individual has to apprehend his own possibility for existence from his direct experience. The history of psychology has seen times when psychologists, sensitive to similar matters, utilized introspection as *the* method of psychology. The problem with introspection was that it was eventually refined to the point where subjects were asked to report on reduced sensations such as the nature of their seeing red or of hearing a high-pitched sound. Thus, although nineteenth century psychologists were sensitive to the importance of an individual's immediate experience, they asked him to refine it into abstracted qualities, which destroyed epistemologically valuable material. The existential context was lost. Eventually introspection was eliminated as technique altogether because it was not objective enough for twentieth century psychologists.

To Husserl, noematic reflection was an attempt to penetrate what is most important in existence. He made a distinction that was essentially Cartesian.

The existence that one experiences is not existence but is a direct immediate experience of one existing in a fashion different from the objects that one experiences. Through noematic reflection, Husserl comes back to the *cogito ergo sum* of Descartes. The mere fact that one can reflect, which is in itself an immediate experience, indicates that one has a direct experience of oneself reflecting as well as oneself being. Other objects in man's immediate experience, such as a table or an orange, clearly do not have this ability.

People communicate to one another in everyday life in a manner that utilizes their nuances and gestures, but ultimately the immediate process that both are undergoing is of greater importance. Even when there is an attempt to communicate an abstract idea as, for example, a point in mathematics or science, there is difficulty in separating what one would like to communicate objectively from one's own nuances of expression based on the context of his life. For science, this is defined as error; for the rest of life, it may be its essence. The legitimacy of phenomenology goes back to the individual for demonstration: One can speak words, attempt to communicate, say that he understands what another is saying, say that he understands that you understand what he is saying, and so forth. This, of course, disallows the possibility of confirmation of ideas the way science confirms them. Ultimately, within the framework of phenomenology, I do not know about your reality or your experience with regard to anything. I can only extend to you from my own experience. Even the science that we can share must emanate from our immediate experience. Science, in a way, is the abstracted distilled commonality in our communication. We cannot be ultimately certain that we share a group of ideas with others. When a human being himself is examined, his direct experience from which science emanates may be of greater importance than the abstraction that science can provide. Thus phenomenal description is the method of dealing with that area of human existence that is excluded by traditional science and philosophy.

I wrote in *Assumptions of Social Psychology* that description is merely prelude to scientific prediction. This is true within a scientific, contingency-oriented epistemology where prediction is the sine qua non. Clearly within the context of a phenomenological system, description is central to understanding.

In phenomenology, the assumptions accompanying a description are either implicit or a part of the description. In empirical psychology, epistemological assumptions are either stated and give direction to the development of the theoretical line or they are implicit and the theorist is unaware of them, which often results in a great deal of wasted effort. Often, a theoretical system will be applied to problems that it cannot logically solve.

Whether it comes from a phenomenological or scientific experimental context, any extended thesis about the nature of man is glib. The saving grace of a given theory is the theorist's knowledge that it is glib. The attempt to apply a given interpretation of an individual's existence from either a scientific or phenomenological point of view, so that it extends to all or most aspects of his existence, requires that the interpretation eventually ask the kind of questions that are better answered by the other major epistemology. We shall see in further chapters that these *reductii ad absurdum* are present in extant psychological theories.

6

Personality Theory

Virtually all personality theories have a sense of self at their epistemological core.[1] The inclusion of the concept of self in a theory is accompanied by an attempt to explain aspects of human existence from the individual's point of view. If self is taken as the core concept of a system, one's place in the world is of central importance. Because most personality theories deal with self, they almost always have a phenomenological quality in much of their conceptualization, even though they may include causal analysis. This phenomenal quality emerges because most personality theories yield psychotherapies that involve a strong sense of immediate experience. This therapeutic by-product is a function of the fact that, historically, clinical psychologists and psychiatrists have developed these theories. As we shall see, the impetus given by Freud was so great as to link psychotherapies with personality theories for many years afterward.

Because personality theories are focused upon a complicated and sometimes illusive concept of self, they run a constant risk of excluding more mundane characteristics which may, nevertheless, be of significance. This limitation is offset by the fact that personality theories have a relevance to experienced life that is often missing in theories of other psychological phenomena.

THE PERSONALITY SYSTEM OF SIGMUND FREUD

Freud worked with many people suffering from classical neurotic symptoms. This directed Freud's interests and theoretical tendencies toward building a personality theory with a derivative psychotherapy that could explain both

---

[1]There are certain methodological positions which do not include the concept. However, they are not technically theories, but rather techniques of therapy.

normal and abnormal behavior (Freud, 1959, 1960a, b). His biological interests as a medical researcher in a variety of other fields were consistent with his assumption that a full understanding of human existence must begin with the most fundamental biological systems of the organism. As we have seen, Nietzsche had already established the importance of the primordial motivational aspects of human existence, a context in which Freud became theoretically comfortable by the early part of the twentieth century. Freud sought the basic motivations of human beings in the appetitive systems. He believed these systems interacted with the immediate social conditions of mother and child given at birth. He combined these observations and developed a causative deterministic system, which sought to enumerate essentially immutable patterns in human development.

We shall see that Freud's biological emphasis in theory and experiential focus in therapy was to confuse many of his critics and supporters. Interestingly enough, the psychotherapy that was derived in part from the system was not necessarily deterministic.

Freud did no experiments, and most of his information about human beings came from his consulting room and from his ability to abstract from the lessons of sociological history and mythology. He was one of the first theorists to consider a vast range of human activity in developing his theory of personality. He emphasized the first few years of life and in so doing provided insights into child development that no one had done before. His arguments concerning the development of an organism were constructed, not from experimentation, but from in situ observation and derivatives from biological givens. In the following section I will borrow liberally from many of Freud's writings and interpret his system in a manner reflecting what I believe to be some of the sounder points in his system.

THE ORIGINAL CONDITION

One of the irrefutable facts about human beings is that when they are born, they are removed from a liquid environment and placed in a gaseous one within the space of hours. The change in environment is a change away from the body of the mother to an environment with no immediate contactual means of support. When a child is born, the mother or mother surrogate must continually see to virtually all of its needs or the infant cannot survive. Growth for humans, as well as for all other animals, is a continuing process of this separation from the original host body of the mother. During the early life of the infant, the mother must feed it, move it from painful situations, pick it up, and give it affection. Although the mother is usually totally indulgent during the first few months of life, she will eventually begin to intensify the process of separation as she must if the child is to take its place in the society of human beings. There is no real alternative to this increasing gap between mother and child since all animals must be more or less separate from one another in order to survive as single entities.[2]

During the process of separation of mother from child, the child seeks to continue the close relationship. It attempts to maintain the status quo since it shows evidence of being quite comfortable with the symbiotic relationship. It resists attempts on the mother's part to block its immediate gratification; she insists that the child perform various activities according to sets of rules derived from the society in which she lives. In Freudian terms, the child is governed principally by id, which is characterized by the pleasure principle, the process whereby an organism attempts to satisfy its biological needs immediately. In turn, the mother or mother surrogate attempts to structure the child's environment so that his ego may develop and so that the reality principle (the ability to delay gratification in order to gain greater satisfaction in the future while experiencing a minimum of punishment or pain) may replace the pleasure principle.

The mother or mother surrogate becomes the principal individual toward whom the child feels love, since she is the origin of nurturance. Since she forces the child to deal with the environment by himself, she is also the object of anger and therefore, potentially, hate. This situation produces the basic life ambivalence which Freud emphasized. An important point is that this ambivalence is biologically given. It is learned, but the learning is inevitable since it is fairly certain that human beings perceive those closest to them ambivalently as both objects of love and of hate. For Freud, this becomes the initial human motivational condition in that individuals are always involvd in the ambivalence of love and hate when other people enter their lives. Depending upon the resolution of this ambivalence for the living of daily life, a person will either be reasonably happy or will find life difficult and oppressive. For the child, this ambivalence is the context for guilt because he feels anger toward a person that he also loves. When this is coupled with the greater acceptibility of the public expression of love compared with hate or anger, guilt will be repressed. The guilt itself eventually gives rise to anxiety. Anxiety comes about as an anticipation of feeling guilty, which is uncomfortable. The possibility for guilt increases sharply when the child begins to internalize the rules of society so that they become his own.

THE DEVELOPMENT OF THE ID, EGO, AND SUPEREGO

In order to determine how Freud handled the motivational consequences of initial ambivalence, we must briefly remind the reader of the notion of the three

[2]Of course, certain types of animals (such as bees and ants) maximize species rather than individual survival.

component parts of the personality system: the id, the ego, and the superego. We shall see how the interaction of these three aspects or processes of the personality preserve ambivalence, which takes the form of oppositional tendencies among couplets of the three. The id refers to the genetically given appetitive systems and the various functions of the body that are controlled directly by the autonomic nervous system. Behaviorally, it is characterized by a tendency to respond immediately and directly to appropriate objects in the environment (pleasure principle). The id, in action, is boldly drawn in animals and in young children. If an infant baby is hungry and food is placed in front of it, it simply grabs at it and stuffs it into its mouth. There are, of course, no social amenities attached to the process, as the child's direct approach to food is accepted by adults. Similar behavior in an older person would be unacceptable. The direct approach of a dog to the presence of meat is tolerated by adults for the same reasons as it is tolerated in children. A very primitive man is characterized in a similar way, so that the development of human beings as a species was taken by Freud to be similar to the development of the single human being from birth to adulthood.

It is during this early period that the child's ambivalence toward the mother grows. The mother is at first tolerant toward the child's forays but becomes increasingly restrictive. These restrictions aid in the formation of the ego. The child's ability to delay gratification and to manipulate the environment so as to maximize rewards while reducing pain is increased. The ego's motivational source is the id in that the ego serves the id in gaining appetitive satisfaction. The difference at this stage is that the ego takes into account the reaction of the world to the individual, while the id does not. Consequently, in the long run, id motivations are more or less served, while the organism is protected from an environment that is potentially hostile.

However, there are oppositional tendencies in the id and ego; since id processes are direct while ego processes are largely indirect, there is always a contradiction between the genetic or physiological motivational conditions of the organism and the exigencies of the world around it. This is also, ultimately, the source of young people's negative reaction to the apparent hypocrisy of the socialized adult who appears to constantly compromise with life. Although there are vast differences in the degree and kind of compromise that adults engage in, it is clear that compromise in the sense of the ego and id juxtaposition is necessary to the life of human beings. There is no alternative to this conflict other than death. Again, the opposition is that preserved from the ambivalence of life in its most basic form, that is, the child's love–hate relationship to the mother.

The third system of the personality, the superego, is a product of the conflict that arises from the ambivalence of feelings toward the mother. The superego is thus the set of internalized rules of procedure and behavior that the individual holds with regard to others in society. These rules are no longer grounded in the exigencies that meet ego. They thus appear to the individual to have no pragmatic basis. The alleviation of guilt is best handled by adherence to these rules. In some instances, these rules are seen to emanate directly from God and and therefore interpreted to be inviolable and unanalyzable. Ego performance, being in the service of the id and therefore pragmatic, cannot be seen as just and correct and guilt alleviating, but somehow must be detached from such a pragmatic basis. The superego is more or less well formed in all people but, of course, will differ greatly in content from culture to culture. The ambivalence between the ego and id, which, as we have seen above, is oppositional, is eased with the formation of the superego, since rules of conduct no longer have a pragmatic basis. However, the superego now maintains a contradictory or conflictual relationship with the id, since it is mainly composed of rules of conduct to control its free expression; the id, being biologically determined, cannot be eliminated but only diverted.

The control of the id by the superego can thus create problems. Since the ego is in service to the id, it also can be in opposition to the superego. The formation of particular personalities, therefore, can be explained by the various oppositional and ambivalent tendencies that exist among these three processes of the personality. Freud pays particular attention to the sexual component of id, because it is the one system that Western society has never been able to handle quite as successfully as the other appetitive processes. It is also the one that most directly involves the childhood ambivalence between mother and child.

As the mother engages in separation attempts, sexual union is the one distinct method for the child of fusing once again with her. The child clearly does not perceive his sexuality in these adult terms, but there is the eroticism of holding and fondling by the mother, which does approximate the state of being in utero or of being close to the mother. The expression of sexual love and its long-term restriction by society until the child is postpubescent creates another difficulty. Freud, for a good part of his career, focused on the various maladaptions of sexual motivation. However, I would prefer to think that the most important concept that Freud held, was the idea of basic ambivalence and oppositional tendencies in human beings, which simply included the sexual among other motives. Carl Gustav Jung and others were to interpret the motivational systems of human beings differently from Freud.

JUNG

Jung's (1956) psychology extended the dialectical or oppositional character of personality as Freud saw it. Jung brought this oppositional character into bold focus while in Freud it remained somewhat peripheral. According to Jung, the pervasive motivational characteristic of human beings can be described by the apparent polar opposites, introversion and extroversion. All individuals can be characterized as being more or less introverted or extroverted. In most people, one dominates, at least slightly. In some instances there is extreme dominance of either introverted or extroverted tendencies and in these cases psychotherapy might be required. Ill health is essentially defined as an extreme imbalance between these two characteristics. In normal relationships one may be more or less introverted or extroverted. Introversion refers to the tendency to turn inward, to seek pursuits that carry an individual away from other individuals and that emphasize one's own devices in dealing with the world. Conversely, extroversion refers to the individual who turns outward toward other people and objects external to his own processes.

Although Jung's system does not have the biological flavor of Freud's, it is clear that it is as deterministic. That is, the tendency toward introversion and extroversion in all people is a precondition for responding in the world. Jung would not deny that they are, in essence, biological givens. What it means to respond in the world is restricted by its nature. This is particularly apparent in Jung's interpretation of the behavior of individuals and of groups (cultures), with regard to a number of universal responses.

Jung accepted the Freudian notion of a personalized unconscious but added as well the idea of a universal and a collective unconscious. The personal unconscious is the product of the particular life of the individual.[3] The collective unconscious is a product of the way individuals in similar cultures have lived over long periods of time. (For example, Southern Europeans appear optimistic in the face of disaster and life in general while Northern Europeans are often pessimistic in similar situations. The difference, for Jung, is due to what it means to live in the easy, sunny warm lands of the southern portion of Europe rather than in the cold North.) The universal unconscious provides the tendency to respond in a similar way by everyone to similar circumstances because of what it means to respond in the world. The universal unconscious is illustrated by the fact that all cultures have a concept of evil that is opposite to that of good. The religions of all cultures include a deity who is connected with evil, and all individuals see part of themselves as evil in a variety of direct and symbolic ways. We shall expand on this theme below.

These various tendencies toward unconscious possibilities for response are not of a genetically transmitted sort, nor are they magical or mystical in any way, but rather simply refer to the ways in which people must respond to their environment because they are human. We see in this point a determinism and biological orientation similar to that of Freud. Jung saw the organism as placed in a context that allowed only certain ranges of possible responses and ideas, these being determined by the individual's own conditions of physiology and

---

[3]He does not emphasize the kinds of influences on its formation that Freud does; i.e., sexuality is minimized.

the particular form of his environment. Even the universal unconscious is presumably an evolved set of response possibilities to an environment that will always have certain characteristics. The idea of good and evil as universal categories is a similar point to the Freudian notion of biologically determined conflict between mother and child. In short, there will always be conflict in an individual, given his nature. One might say at this point that the Jungian notion of a universally held concept of good and evil is a more generalized extension of Freud's idea of the conflict of positive and negative responses that the child naturally must feel toward its mother.

Jung noted that one cannot constantly be good or do good without contemplating and holding in oneself the concept of evil. To the extent that human beings contemplate evil, they become, in part, evil. At least they see the possibilities for evil as well as for good in themselves. Consequently, good and evil become an oppositional set of forces to be striven for and to be striven against. Society indirectly glorifies the evil side of man by making heros of those who break laws that few deny are good. The individual who drives an automobile recklessly or who is callous in his relationship with women is a potential hero figure in Western society, yet at the same time no one would deny that the rules of conduct that define that individual as reckless and callous are good in themselves. It is Jung's contention that awareness that these oppositional motivational factors do indeed exist in oneself, in one's culture, and in human beings in general, is essential to mental health. With this realization, people can obtain a balance in their lives between oppositional forces and can perceive others as requiring a similar equilibrium.

ANIMA AND ANIMUS

One of the most important oppositional dichotomies found in Jung is that between Animus, the male spirit, and Anima, the female spirit. This characteristic is universal. Indeed, in the Orient, it is one of the most important concepts applied to the nature of human beings. Animus, the male principle, is characterized by aggressiveness toward nature and an orientation toward external objects and action rather than thought or emotion. Anima is characterized by subjective internal processes with emphasis on contemplation and emotion rather than action. The epistemological parallel to the introversion–extroversion dichotomy is clear.

This sexual polarity, which Jung has identified as one of the principal dichotomies in human existence, reflects the intimate functional relationship that has always existed among males and females. Over evolutionary time the work and, therefore, the sensitivities of males and females have needed to differ along certain key aspects in order to maintain human existence. Physiological differences between the two have also contributed to male and female separateness. However, one of the most basic principles of animus and anima is that each tendency is contained within the same individual whether male or female. The dominance of animus in a male and anima in a female simply means that their roles are well-established and their opposite component is less strong. Psychological ill health is defined as an excess of one of these tendencies.

Jung noted that American society in particular was uncomfortable with a display of anima in males and of animus in females and that this is an aberrant aspect of the culture. An example of this is expressed by Jung in his observation that Americans cannot see shoemakers as poets nor poets as shoemakers. This is particularly evident with a group of professional athletes whose occasional member, becoming interested in literature or painting, is seen as a strange bird. With athletes one finds what might be conceived as the stereotypic extreme of animus such that any display of anima is looked upon with suspicion. The same holds true for a woman who becomes an athlete. She is often looked upon with equal suspicion. It is clear, however, that, particularly with regard to females, the acceptable balance of anima and animus may be shifting because of the sensibilities that have arisen in women as a result of the women's liberation movement.

Jung's motivational aspects of personality, although differing in emphasis from Freud, are not inconsistent with them. Actually, the psychotherapies of both men are different, but the theoretical structure remains similar (and deterministic). Hence, Jung's concepts, like Freud's, are essentially analytic. However, like Freud's, his psychotherapy is existential in nature.

EXISTENTIAL PSYCHOLOGY

Existential psychology, manifested mainly via the clinical area, is a derivative of phenomenology. It focuses upon the person as he emerges and becomes in the world. The major feature of an existential psychology, and particularly an existential psychotherapy, is that the individual is considered essentially free; that is, he has responsibility for himself and can be or become virtually anything he wishes. It is the therapist's job to help him realize that he is free and that he therefore can make a variety of choices. No presuppositions are made about the nature of the individual or his motivation, but rather his immediate experience is dealt with directly by both therapist and patient. Psychologists must constantly examine their own presuppositions so as to describe accurately the life of the patient. They must avoid abstractions and instead describe what he is at the time.

Most difficulties encountered in psychotherapy are attributable to an individual's experience rather than to his behavior or to the structure of his personality. The development of one's sense of self in a manner that makes one satisfied and happy is the goal of existential psychotherapy. This principle of self-actualization is central in the systems of Abraham Maslow (1962), Carl Rogers (1942), and others. For Rogers it was important whether the individual sees himself as being someone that he would like to be or someone with whom he is dissatisfied. Health implies that an individual is and becomes who he wants to be. The healthy person knows that there is congruence between health and experience; there is an openness to experience and defensiveness is minimum. The neurotic individual is one whose self-concept is not consistent with his organismic experience. He is characterized by denial and defense.

Existential theories of psychology are nonmotivational as compared with psychoanalytic theories. Motivational concepts, as we have seen earlier, are causal in nature, and this is contradictory to the basic existential assumption that immediate experience is central in dealing with human beings.

THEORY AND THERAPY

Freud and Jung represent personality theory's classical tradition. In addition to these, which have been explained briefly above, I would like to examine three ultracontemporary systems of personality that seem to be most popular today. They are the cognitive theory of George Kelly, the primal theory of Arthur Janov, and the transactional analysis of Eric Berne. In so doing, I will attempt to show that each of these are variations of two basic epistemological themes in personality theory, although the therapeutic varieties are endless. Epistemologically, there are very few interpretations of the nature of the whole personality. Other modern theories could have been substituted for these with the same epistemological result. Other systems include the various developments from Freudian psychoanalysis such as the theories of Harry Stack Sullivan (1953), the neo-Freudians, and Otto Rank (1929)—also, the social learning of Julian Rotter (1954), the trait factor-analytic approach of Raymond B. Cattell (1965), and Bandura's (1969) variations on behavior modification, as well as Wolpe's (1958) classical conditioning approach.

The imagination of most theorists seems to have gone into developing a variety of therapeutic techniques rather than into attempts to construct theoretical insights into the nature of human beings. This is understandable since the latter activity is much more difficult.

THE TRANSACTIONAL ANALYSIS OF ERIC BERNE

Like many modern theories, transactional analysis (Berne, 1961) is based on dealing with conscious ego states, although there are Freudianlike implications that these are connected to the usual repressed and unconscious motivations discussed in psychoanalytic theory. Berne's system depends upon structural analysis that involves the separation of discreet ego states. Within this framework, therapy and cure take place. Like many modern therapies, the analyst fully informs the patient as to what he is attempting and what the process is in which they are both engaged. Abstract intelligence regarding oneself and others is acceptable and, indeed, preferable to uninformed emotion. Berne believes that transactional analysis, like psychoanalysis, allows the expression of genuine affect rather than encouraging emotive outbursts based on immediate traumatic experience. He made a distinction among the concepts of superego, ego, and id and between ego states that are experiential and behavioral realities. Hence, there is a tendency to translate the Freudian superego, ego, and id into parent, adult, and child as operative nomenclature for transactional analysis.

The idea is that the Freudian terminology refers to inferred concepts, whereas familial labels represent actual existential states corresponding to real people. This appears to be a therapeutic strategy rather than a real difference between Berne's and Freud's concepts. Therapy corresponds to the three types of ego states. With certain types of schizophrenics, the therapist may have to play a parental role and can thus exhibit a parental ego state with certain advantage. In working with adults, he can most efficiently use an adult ego state, and in play therapy with children a child ego state is most appropriate.

For individuals that are likely to benefit from this treatment, a similar type of structural analysis is made; that is, every human being responds to the environment around him within the framework of parental, adult, or child ego states. All of his behavior can be classified into those three categories. Again, the dubious distinction is made that superego, ego, and id are inferential concepts, while ego states are experiential. This may be a distinction without a difference. It is also assumed that all three of these ego states are potentially fully developed in any adult. Berne suggested that the problem may arise that only one or more of these states may be "weakly" cathected. Maturity and immaturity are eliminated as appropriate labels for explaining any particular type of behavior, but rather it is conceived that an individual may use a child ego state more frequently than an adult ego state. Berne's constant reminder has been that transactional analysis has a behavioral existential focus, as opposed to the conceptual states of psychoanalysis implied in the use of such terms as superego, ego, and id.

Transactional analysis thus is an attempt to understand which ego state is active in any given exchange among two or more people. Various patterns of interactions (adult to child, child to parent, and so forth) form the potential dynamic for communication among people and therefore the basis for either health or sickness. Presumably, "people's adult" speaking to other people's adult, people's child speaking to child, and so forth, is healthier than people's adult speaking to child, and so forth.

Berne also concentrated on what he called game analysis, which is a series of transactions among individuals with ulterior motives. This concept is carried over to what is called script analysis where an unconscious life plan may come to light.

The transactional theory of personality represented only minor variations on the Freudian notion of the development of id, ego, and superego. The first five years of life was of extreme importance for Berne as it was for Freud, and the early relationships among child and parents were considered "early transactions." Although labeling it differently, Berne stressed the conflict that is central to Freud's thinking. Transactions apparently arise from, or are part of, conflict. This conflict, as we have seen, stems from the necessary separation of child from mother, which commences early in life. Because Berne focused upon child and adult problems, he did not particularly emphasize the inevitability of conflict but rather its amenability to correction via his own particular type of therapy.

Berne accepted the idea that a turning point in the growth of a child occurs when he comes to understand that he cannot have everything he wants and that he must control himself and meet the demands of other people. This can be characterized as the pleasure principle giving way to the reality principle. The "games" that Berne frequently referred to, can also be described as leitmotifs of which, again, Freud was cognizant in his sensitivity to arrested development initiated during the various psychosexual stages. For example, stress during the oral or anal periods could influence the structure of an individual personality throughout life. Most of Berne's system, although discussed under the guise of theory, is really a set of therapeutic techniques or interpretations of behavioral possibilities and as such adds little to personality theory.

THE PRIMAL THERAPY OF ARTHUR JANOV

Transactional analysis focuses on the cognitive interchange among people, resulting in generalizations and abstractions about behavior. Janov's (1970) primal therapy focuses on feeling as basic reality and neurosis as a disease of feeling. Abstractions and intellectualizations get in the way of effecting a cure for neurosis. Virtually all interpretations of his own behavior are the neurotic's defenses, which must be removed. The healthiest individual is the individual who is defense free. Neurotic defense systems against the world are both internal and external. These defense systems lie deep in neurosis and insulate neurotic tension which cannot, therefore, be expiated. It is the release of neurotic tension built up over the years to specific life instances that is linked with health. Hence, Janov also has, at base, a Freudianlike conflict model of neurosis and, indeed, of existence. As does Freud, he espouses a tension-release model as basic to therapy. Whereas for Freud catharsis is part but not parcel of therapy, this deep release of tension for Janov is its essence. However, this is not to be confused with simple catharsis in the Freudian sense, as we shall see.

Human infants cannot deal with their own needs directly. For Janov, it follows that the infant must therefore separate these needs (hunger, thirst, love) from consciousness. That is, he must make them unconscious. This he calls the *split*. The organism creates this split in order to protect itself against nonfulfillment. This is nothing more than the Freudian conflict model yielding motivations that have become unconscious to the individual. These needs continue to act throughout the entire life of the individual depending on how severely they have been restricted.

A certain type of shattering occurs in a child's life, which is called the primal scene. There are two types: major and minor. The major primal scene is a single traumatic event that is accompanied by existential loneliness, a feeling of separateness, and deep bitterness. Before this major primal scene occurs, there might be any number of minor primal scenes in which the process of separation into loneliness is begun by a series of events that continually separate a child from others. Janov, as well as Berne, did not particularly differentiate between this process of separation accompanied by rejection or neglect on the part of an adult, and separation accompanied by love. This is a crucial distinction that Janov did not recognize. Neuroses are fostered by this split as is the constant life-long need for love of the mother or mother surrogate.

The discovery of the primal scream occurred when Janov witnessed one of his patients cry out "mommy" and issue a scream that was unlike any Janov had heard before. He was convinced it was not simply catharsis, but something more basic. After the primal scream, the individual felt much better. The primal scene is extremely painful and the child turns away form the full realization of what has happened, namely, a culmination of the "split." Hence, this realization becomes unconscious, but, in the Freudian sense of repressed material, is active throughout the remainder of the individual's life. Associated with this primal conflict is the possibility of eventually getting the patient to consciously talk directly to the people (that is, mother or father) who caused this basic psychic pain — to scream at them in a direct way telling them they were the agents of hurt. The scream itself comes from the noncivilized, nonabstracted, pure emotional expression of pain. With this release, the neurotic is well on his way to cure.

Trauma obviously plays a central role in Janov's system. Consequently, birth itself provides the initial possibility for the trauma à la Otto Rank. Janov concluded that all births are not traumatic, contrary to Rank, but traumatic births *are* traumatic and hence the primal situation can begin even at that point. The primal scream itself is not simply catharsis, as we have mentioned, nor simple tension-release, as is implicit in the notion of catharsis, but rather is in itself a "curative process." The scream is an expression of pain and the felt pain allows the repressed feelings that led to its storage to finally surface and be dissipated. Hence, repression also plays a central part in Janov's system, as it did in Freud's.

The initial pains of childhood enacted in primal scenes become deeply stored tension and the only way to bring about release is to eventually recreate the primals and allow the stored or repressed emotion out in an explosive manner. Primals, when they are reached in therapy, contain no abstraction, no reasoning, and no verbalization. They are sheer emotive feeling. Primal therapy, according to Janov, is not an interactive process but rather is an unfolding of an individual's insight, which does not particularly involve other people at the time. Interestingly enough, both Janov's and Berne's systems have strong existential components, although transactional analysis has elements that overlap the operant notions of behavior motification. Janov remained more consistent with the Freudian emphasis on catharsis, but without the interpretive aspect of therapy upon which Freud focused.

THE PERSONAL CONSTRUCT THEORY
OF GEORGE A. KELLY

Kelly's (1955) major assumption about man was that he can be best characterized by his efforts to conceptualize his environment; that is, his conceptualizations are designed to predict behavior for himself and others and to allow him to proceed to satisfy as many goals as he can in life. Kelly believed that this attempt was conscious. His approach is experimental in the sense that individuals make guesses about what is true about their environment. In short, man acts as a scientist acts, and like a scientist he sometimes fails in constructing correct hypotheses within his own abstracted framework about the nature of life. Thus man attempts to order phenomena on the basis of his own constructs. This framework allows him to anticipate or predict what might be true about life.

Clearly, in simple situations all people succeed in predicting correctly about life. They can predict successfully that a building marked "Post Office" will, in most instances, accept letters that they wish to mail. Man thus is able to represent the environment in cognition. He is not simply a responder to the environment, as a number of other personality systems would have it, but is a cognizer. The development of the personal constructs system allows an individual freedom of choice but also limits action, because an individual's chosen constructs define his response possibilities. That is, he is limited by the responses he can make by having chosen those constructs rather than some others. The constructs system allows him to inject meaning into the world rather than to simply respond to the stimulation around him. By rejecting formerly held constructs and accepting others, he regains his freedom but then, of course, takes on an immediate limitation as well.

This is very much a phenomenological, indeed, existential position. There is no objective reality or absolute truth that is discoverable concerning human beings. Rather, a human being simply attempts to make sense out of events for himself. Science itself is not a pursuit of truth, but a pursuit of useful ways of dealing with the universe. Subjectivism, therefore, is layered within science, a point made earlier.

Kelly recognized that psychologists, and indeed all scientists, do not always ask the most important questions about human existence particularly via the clinical method—the clinical method, in this case, being any direct approach to individuals who come to a clinical psychologist with problems about existence, which the psychologist recognizes as such. Fear of not being scientific, as a great many psychologists are, has allowed many of them to successfully avoid dealing with significant problems of existence.

Kelly's idea of construct is not dissimilar to the old ideas of attitude, *einstellung,* or set. At least in terms of its function, the construct allows an individual to make abstractions without examining every single event in a given class that confronts him. Such an idea is virtually the definition of an attitude, if one also includes an emotive element. In concepts like attitude, personal construct, and set, we find the idea of cognitive and emotive generalization. The process of generalization, in whatever form, is one that has allowed people to deal with daily events with some degree of success, but also, of course, has led them into prejudices and other incorrect generalizations.

The idea of constructs includes a similarity and a contrast polarity. There are three necessary elements in a construct: two of the elements need to be perceived as similar to each other and the third as different from the other two (a dialectical form). In this respect, Kelly shared a fundamental epistemological notion with Freud, Jung, Janov, Berne, and others. Kelly substituted for the unconscious–conscious dichotomy of psychoanalysts a verbal–preverbal construct. However, this substitution added but little to the clarity of the older unconscious–conscious polarity. Understanding a human being as a therapeutic problem coincides with knowledge of the constructs employed by that individual in dealing with the world. This is the sine qua non for therapy and for understanding.

Kelly's techniques of therapy involve specific role figures that are most likely to play a part in the life of an individual such as the father and mother. The way an individual sees these people and the way he reacts to them in various combinations allows the therapist to grasp the kinds of constructs he employs.

Anxiety is considered to be an individual's recognition that leading events in his life lie outside the range of his construct system. Guilt, also, is a kind of psychological separation from one's basic roles in life and does not involve a superego. The distinction Kelly made between his interpretation of guilt and Freud's seems to be minor, since the Freudian superego referred to a sense of self-definition as much as a personal construct does. Indeed, the superego might be thought of as a personal construct even though determined by cultural factors.

What Kelly eliminated from his system, but which Freud included, is the origins of certain forms of constructlike systems such as the superego. Indeed, one of the great weaknesses of Kelly's system is that he said little about the nature and motivations of the kinds of constructs that people have in common. Freud's epistemological intent, therefore, was deeper than Kelly's in that basic origins of constructlike concepts are sought in even more basic concepts. The notion of superego is more encompassing than Kelly's construct of guilt, which he substitutes for it.

Psychotherapy for Kelly is a process where an individual is aided in improving his predictions about the nature of his life and is therefore helped in changing his constructs in order to make better predictions. Thus *becoming* is a central idea for Kelly. Psychology is the reconstruction of life concepts, an idea consistent with phenomenological and existential positions already discussed.

GENERAL COMMENT

It is clear that, with the exception of behavior modification, virtually all personality theories do not follow the causal scientific model as we have described it. The objective scientific model has not been successful when applied to the psychotherapeutic situation. In instances where a causal model, for example, Freud's, has been used, the psychotherapy that accompanies it has depended upon the nature of the immediate experience of the individual and on interaction *at the time of therapy* between patient and therapist.

In the past, the therapeutic situation, in its immediacy, has often been thought of as a temporary expedient that allows the therapist to deal with the patient's difficulty but is independent of the development of concepts. The phenomenologist and others have pointed out that the rough and ready therapeutic approach of most clinical psychologists does contain the seed of a true insight into the nature of human beings; namely, that immediate experience can be dealt with only in its own terms and not through those of the causal scientific model. Thus, although personality theory has often had causal lines imbedded within it, there has always been that "extra ingredient" that made these theories very different in form, method, and concepts from those found in other areas of psychology. In part, the reason for this is that personality theorists have implicitly or explicitly recognized the essential phenomenal quality with which they were dealing in the interactive therapeutic situation.

7

Social Theory

All theories of social activity include the supposition that an individual's experience is, in large part, influenced by his relationships with other people. Therefore, all social psychological theories are, at base, psychologies of the single individual expanded to deal with his activity in groups. Historically, there have been social theories that developed the concept of an emerging group mind, but these have largely fallen into disrepute. Most theories of social existence are of the deterministic predictive type. One of the great difficulties in demonstrating the effectiveness or correctness of any given system within the context of an actual social situation is that experiments utilized to develop theory are more unlike actual social situations than perhaps most other forms of experiments on human beings. Coupled with this is the fact that social activity is so complex, and the motivational structures involved so vast, that it is extraordinarily difficult to make successful predictions within the framework of a single theoretical line.

Over the past several years, social psychologists have developed a good working knowledge of the way that attitudes and opinions are formed, changed, and manifested behaviorally. However, it remains extremely difficult actually to utilize this knowledge to change attitudes in a given social context. As we saw in Chapter 4, the difficulty arises because there are so many other factors operative besides attitudes that determine social behavior.

Theoretical approaches in social psychology follow the same epistemological paths as do theories in personality or developmental psychology. There has been a strong objective tradition in social psychology centering on reinforcement and drive reduction theory as well as the development of a Gestalt field-theoretical position. However, the unique quality that is presented by the subject matter of social psychological theories yields certain shifts in epistemological emphasis. Freud understood that the psychology of the individual personality was at one with the psychology of the individual as a social being. In that sense personality theory and social psychological theory are the same.

However, while personality theory continued to focus on the individual within the context of the nuclear family, social psychology made an attempt to deal with the individual in the socio-economic political group. This almost always extended beyond the nuclear family, and (although sometimes maintained in small groups), required that the unit under investigation transcend the usual familial relationships. This conception eventually gave way to two possibilities: examining the individual as he reacted to being part of the group and how this influenced his perception and learning, and examining the reaction of the individual to the fact of group membership. Hence the initial problem for social psychology has been the study of the nature of the formation and change of attitudes and beliefs.

An attitude itself requires the ability to discriminate among various social stimuli as well as the ability to form perceptual and response generalizations regarding various social stimulus classes. Hence, an attitude is often defined as an emotive response of liking or disliking an identifiable class of stimuli, usually social in nature. This conception of attitude lent itself to the formation of theories that were based on reinforcement, social learning, or exchange theory.

The epistemological bases of these types of theories are the same as those of similar theories found in personality and learning. They are objective and are dependent on experimentation for confirmation. In reinforcement-type theories, the attitude concept is eliminated and a concentration on the functional relation between stimulus class input and opinion output is substituted without theoretical reference. Nevertheless, the epistemological assumptions remain the same, namely, that it is possible to develop theories about reaction to social stimuli on the basis of discrimination and generalization through experimentation. Related to these reinforcement-based theories are cognitive consistency theories that depend upon the notion of a tendency toward reaching an equilibrium (a motivational concept) among certain forms of cognitive behavior. The basic difference in, for example, Festinger's cognitive dissonance theory (Festinger, 1957) and early reinforcement theory is the focus upon conscious thought processes rather than upon more peripherially activated responses. It is not our intention to discuss these types of theories here since they have been extensively discussed elsewhere (e.g., Shaw & Constanzo, 1970; M. Deutsch & Krauss, 1965).

I have selected Berger and Luckmann, role theory, and the exchange theory of Uriel and Edna Foa for a detailed analysis of social theories in terms of their epistemological assumptions. Berger and Luckmann are included as an example of the phenomenological approach to social explanation. Role theory is included because it represents a set of data that is not typically handled by the usual concepts of social psychology. The Foas' system is included as one of the ultracurrent attempts at theory that incorporate many of the points of earlier reinforcement, field, and cognitive theories.

BERGER AND LUCKMANN

In the phenomenological tradition, Berger and Luckmann's (1966) system attempts to explain social phenomena in a manner that epistemologically fuses objective and subjective social reality. In order to accomplish this task their theory needs not only to encompass, but also to extend beyond, the devices of the natural sciences. Common sense experience of the social world can only be dealt with by techniques foreign to the natural sciences.

There is no question but that the nature of the various institutions of cooperation and social order provide an objective context in which individuals find themselves. Berger and Luckmann described the habitual arrangements human beings make in order to live with one another. This description is of prime importance since there is remarkable similarity among basic social orders even in culturally diverse peoples. There are always, for example, familial relationships with well-defined roles and behavioral expectancies, policing functions, and gods.

Social institutions develop by reciprocal habitualizations among people over similar issues. These habitualizations act as determiners of social activity. However, causal explanations of social phenomena are limited. Hence, description becomes crucial since Berger and Luckmann dealt with myths, superstitions, religions, and other slowly evolved social entities. Explaining the social use of myths, including religion, requires that the theorist has already explicitly or implicitly decided to deal with social phenomena as he found them, with no attempt to reduce description to simple principles. More reductionistic analysis of myths and religions always yield conclusions that involve behavioral reinforcement with what are considered basic biological processes such as fear, hunger, or sex, as in Freud's idea that religion is a way of dealing with certain manifestations of fear.

The dialectic between subject and object within the context of social reality is the epistemological model that both arises from this reality and influences it once it is formed. Berger and Luckmann noted that demonic possession in Haiti and neurosis in New York arise from specific social and individual contexts. In turn, the nomenclatures of Freudian analysis and voodoo influence the onset of neurosis and possession. Consequently, a Haitian might very well be possessed and a New York intellectual might very well be neurotic. The objective conditions of a particular society fuse with the individual's subjective "common sense" view of it. We must understand both objective and subjective conditions in order to understand a given social phenomenon. From a strictly objective point of view, it may be argued that a different set of reinforcement contingencies produce a certain type of response in the Haitian compared with the New Yorker.

The question then becomes, what does one know that was not known before a reinforcement analysis? Is a reinforcement explanation in this context circular? In contrast, is there a level at which a dialectic can be introduced that reflects societal customs and individual reaction to those customs, and that yields more information than an explanation that depends upon reinforcement contingencies? Imbedded in this dilemma is the question of whether one can locate reinforcement contingencies that produce either neurosis or possession and whether this can be done without already knowing what to look for?

If we were Skinnerian modelers in Haiti, it would be necessary to have already described a societal condition that served as the context in which we would have then looked for appropriate reinforcements. We would have had to do a bit of sociology—we would have had to look into the history of the rites of voodoo. To look for a reinforcement contingency indicates that one has already utilized a rather complex form of description that is, in part, a description of subjective states. The implication is that as much or more information would have already been gathered before a reinforcement contingency was discovered.

In social situations, it is necessary to understand what has already happened in order to predict what might have happened. That is, of course, what prediction means in science, but when dealing with social phenomena, repetition of events is virtually impossible. Skinner, for one, recognized this and thus suggested that what we should do to produce the society we want is to start from the beginning. Even reconstructing a culture by using the principle of reinforcement raises more problems than it solves, as we have seen in previous chapters. Contingency analyses may be applied to very specific problems, such as teaching a child to read, but cannot illuminate the nature of social existence. Phenomenologists see reinforcement as a superficial description of existence, which leaves untouched many layers of being.[1]

Thus Berger and Luckmann concluded that reality is socially constructed and that objective reality is based upon various levels of agreement among individuals as they live together. Knowledge is a matter of social definition and

---

[1]The argument has been made that societies are the way they are because that is the only way they can be. The reader will recognize the Leibnizian metaphysic in this position. The Vichean idea that all societies develop independently of one another, and only appear to be influenced by one another, is consistent with this Leibnizian concept. Since we know that Vico influenced Marx and Jung in their concepts of inevitable social and unconscious evolutions, respectively, a distinct line of explanatory attack emerges. These positions reflect a concept of structure which, as we shall see in the next chapter, is brought to fruition by Piaget.

refers to what is socially defined as reality and not to some extra social criteria of validity.

The concept of role is of central importance to social definition since it is defined by institutional content. Once an individual accepts a role position, his actions are more or less determined and the sanctions against deviating from that role are more or less set. The concept of role is also a matter of social definition and is consequently relative to the society that constructs it. One role, or institutional reality, cannot be judged better or worse than another role, or institutional reality, unless the assumptions and bases on which the two roles or institutions are based are the same. Interestingly, the same is true for logic. There is a Western European logic, an Eastern logic, an African logic, and so forth. It is not possible for the logic associated with ordinary causal deterministic Western science to be imposed upon the life context of, for example, a central African, unless he accepts the premises and goals of Western European scientific logic. To do this he must, in part, leave his own society either actually or figuratively and enter into a Western European context.

All institutions and roles are verified to a greater or lesser extent by all participants. That portion of self-consciousness that has been objectified is then apprehended as inevitable and the individual disclaims responsibility for his action within that role. For example, if a husband catches his wife in bed with another man, he may, on becoming furious, decide rather quickly that his role as a husband demands that he destroy the man and that he has *no choice* in the matter. Thus, in this instance the social role completely dominates the individual's self-perception of himself; that is, he is at that moment totally determined by the role that he plays. It is also possible for self-identity to be rarified to such a degree that the individual totally identifies himself with his socially assigned typification and is apprehended by others as nothing but a "type." This might be perceived as largely positive or negative depending on his own and others' values.

The institutional order, including its roles, becomes a shield against chaos for its participants. The objectified institutional role is subjectively accepted by an individual to the extent that it protects against the terror of chaos (meaninglessness and death). When society is sufficiently industrialized and has developed to the point where discrepant worlds of being are generally available on virtually a market basis, then there will be an increase in the belief in the relativity of all worlds, including one's own. Following from this, there is an increasing consciousness that one is playing a role within certain aspects of society. Hence, one not only *is,* but one *plays* a role as a student, teacher, or father.

Society as subjective reality.   No one ever completely internalizes the totality of what is objective about his society even though it be a simple one. There are also elements of subjective reality that have not originated in socialization as, for example, the awareness of one's own body. Consequently, an individual apprehends himself as being both inside and outside of society. Although an individual's identity is formed by society during social relations, it is also seen by the individual to stand in juxtaposition to society, producing a constant interchange (dialectic) between the two. This implies an interaction between the subjective self and the objective characteristics of society, as the individual has internalized them. From a developmental perspective, it is evident that the child semiautomatically internalizes the characteristics of his parents and perceives their world as the only world, since he has no other points of comparison.

Psychological theory within this conception of subjective reality is relative to the social definitions of reality and, of course, is itself socially defined. Theory is adequate or not, independent of its empirical scientific character but dependent upon its relative use within a given social context. We shall return to this issue again in Chapter 10.

Mythology. An example of the kind of analysis Berger and Luckmann made, which combines subjective and objective reality already discussed, is illustrated by their description of the nature of mythology. Mythology is defined as "a conception of reality that posits the ongoing penetration of the world of everyday experience by sacred forces [p. 110]." It is clear that there needs to be a high degree of continuity between social and cosmic order.

Theological thought is distinguished from mythology in terms of its greater degree of theoretical systematization. This entails the removal of naiveté from theological thought. The nature of mythology is that it is understandable by all people in a society, from the priest class to the commoner. Religion, with its abstracted conceptual and highly systematized series of tenets, was clearly not understandable to all people and the priest class became the interpreters to the common people of the cosmos and, therefore, of the social order. This is the period in the development of a society where the priest class attained its greatest power, since its members are needed to interpret the cosmic order in relation to the social order. Any rebellious or heterodoxical threat to social definitions of reality is neutralized by assigning it inferior ontological and frivolous intellectual status. This is usually done by defining a threatening group or individual holding heterodoxical beliefs as less than human. This includes what ordinarily has been called the mentally ill who, however, are thought to be generally rehabilitatable.

Eventually, society spawns a priestlike class that is not tied to theology or myth. These are the experts in various fields such as science and, more importantly, experts in the conditions of society itself. They, like the priests, deal in such abstract qualities that they are considered a class apart and need to interpret the existence of society to its members. The assumption is widely held that their theoretical interpretations of society are uninfluenced by societal conditions. This, according to Berger and Luckmann, is an illusion but has great sociohistorical potency since interpretations of reality can sometimes be changed by the interaction of sociocultural forces with abstractions about them. When members of a given society begin to see forces outside of their own culture as comfortable rather than strange, the experts and governors of that society call for direct military action against their own populace. Failing that, they enter into negotiations with the opposition. From this, new cultural mores, folkways, and customs develop and the process repeats itself in dialectic fashion.

ROLE THEORY

Two of the most recent compendia of theories of social psychology (Deutsch & Krauss, 1965; Shaw & Costanzo, 1970) made very similar conclusions about the nature of role theory. Both contended that the concept of role is unique and relatively unclassifiable within the framework of other theories of social psychology that fit more easily into the objective scientific mold of either the reinforcement or field theory variety. The heuristic richness of role concepts is acknowledged by both sources. Yet distance from a scientific ideal is also acknowledged. Role theory seems to have a transitional position between traditional objective approaches to an analysis of social behavior and a phenomenal approach to the same subject matter. The concept of role is, of course, ancient and has existed as a major concept in social psychological theory, at least since the turn of the century.

The idea of role in human social existence encompasses the core of social meaning for the individual. Therefore, the entire idea of self as discussed within the framework of personality theory is a central concept to role theory as well. In role theory, *self* refers to the consistent aspects of a relationship to others in a variety of similar situations. In short, social meaning itself coincides with the concept of role. Roles are located within a status system. Statuses gain meaning only in terms of their purposes relative to one another. Thus, a high status is dependent upon a number of other statuses perceived as lower. Each status has well-defined roles or sets of behavioral expectations, which include behavior expressed by the individual in the role set as well as behavior he may expect to receive. A father provides for the physical needs of a child and gives affection. In turn, he receives love, respect, and obedience.

There are ascribed statuses that are determined by events independent of an individual's choice, such as old, Catholic, or male. There are achieved statuses that are gained by what an individual is capable of doing. For example, occupational roles all have a status assigned to them. The president of a bank has a higher status than a bank guard. Each of these statuses have various roles (role set) assigned to them, such as the terms of address used by the president and the guard to one another. Most role theorists do not attempt to make specific predictions from role descriptions although some are implicit; for example, certain behaviors of an individual maintaining the role of a physician are highly predictable.

Not only do individuals respond in characteristic ways to social situations, but they do so in a way that identifies their sense of center or self with the surrounding society's conception of them acting within a specific social situation. Role theorists of whatever persuasion (George Herbert Mead, 1934; Erving Goffman, 1959; Robert Merton, 1957) base their systems on a description of this self–role juxtaposition. This in turn implies that role theory, as do most social psychological theories, assumes that the acquisition of the concepts of self and role have already been achieved presumably through a process that is described by other subfields of psychology such as learning, perception, motivation, and personality. The unique aspect of the role concept involves expectations of one individual of the behavior of another, given certain information such as occupation and status, which in turn can be catalogued by various types of sociological description. Role theory thus seems to lie between objective and phenomenological social theories.

There is no question that roles are learned. There is some question that a sense of self is learned, however (see Chapter 4). It is interesting to note that even though one may understand fully the way a role is acquired, there is still more information to be added by describing the role itself as it is perceived by the individual and hence, as it involves singular expectations. Since role theory lies outside of the framework of the usual objective experimental model, it is greeted with a great deal of confusion on the part of the catalogers of social psychological theories. The confusion exists because the description found within role theory is very close to the experienced behavior of the individual living within a role structure. Consequently, it is very similar to a phenomenal description of actual behavior.

For example, the father acting as father can be and often is very much aware of that particular position; namely, he feels like a father, he acts like a father, he believes he should act like a father, and he is aware of all of this, at the same time. In short, he is experiencing fatherhood. Role theory attempts to abstract the common characteristic from this felt experience, remaining as close to the original as possible. This in turn disallows the usual objective approach. If the analyzers of social theories are confused about the nature of role theory it is because they have not recognized an essentially phenomenal concept with its accompanying methods and theory, in contrast to the objective experimental character of most other social psychological concepts, methods, and theory.

FOA AND FOA

The most contemporary integrative social psychological theory is that developed by Foa and Foa (1974). The system is extensive and attempts to explain the basis of all social interaction. It is rare in contemporary psychology that such an inclusive attempt is made at all. As we have indicated above, theories in social psychology are more likely to attempt to explain certain circumscribed aspects of human interaction. One of the most interesting aspects of the theory of Foa and Foa is that it conceptually includes many explanatory levels of previously developed theories of social interaction. Reinforcement theory, certain cognitive theories, the ideas of homeostasis and structure are all included as major elements in Foa and Foa's integrative approach. This fact alone provides a number of epistemological levels that can be examined in juxtaposition within the same system, a possibility missing from most other interpretations of social interaction.

There are three major epistemological elements in Foa and Foa's theory: the ideas of structure, functional reinforcement, and cognitive organization. Although these are not necessarily mutually exclusive, we shall see how all three are used to represent different but related levels of understanding.

Structure is defined somewhat differently by various theorists but does have a consistent core of meaning. Foa and Foa (1974) defined it as "a configuration of variables or classes in a space of stated coordinates [p. 10]." The implication is that a defined set of classes have dynamic properties in determining a variety of behaviors that could not be as well-predicted from elements in these classes taken independently of their configural relationships. We have pointed out that the structural base of biochemistry via discoveries concerning the nature of DNA is consistent with certain interpretations of the nature of language. If we consider that language has a structural property in much the same sense as DNA, then there is a rich possibility for the existence of other psychological structures.

Foa and Foa pointed out that information is conveyed by structure. It remains to discover the developmental sequence that yields a particular structure, the nature of that structure, and its influence on human reaction. The Foas lean toward the general idea that structures are formed in a variety of social contexts requiring classical reinforcement. The resulting structure can be cognitive in nature and this in turn can influence future behavior. Thus reinforcement alone, or the existence of cognitive structures alone, cannot account fully for human behavior. Cognitive structure implies an analysis of meaning and this, as we have seen, requires more than a simple functional contingency among words. The authors indicated that certain traditional functional views have fallen short of adequate prediction and explanation because they have not considered structural elements in the organism. Function and structure are not separable concepts in analyzing a coherent behavior sequence, although this error of separation has often been made in modern psychology.

The idea of human structure necessarily implies that it has been developed over time from birth onward. Consequently, any structural theory of human existence needs to be, in part, developmental. Foa and Foa's conception of the development of early structure coincides with that of Piaget. Differentiation and generalization are related processes absolutely necessary to the development of more complex structures. Initially, an infant responds to all adults in a similar manner. Only later does he differentiate father from all men and mother from all women. The development of the ability to discriminate eventually leads to the ability to place these discriminated stimuli in classes, which is a process of generalization. The empirical evidence concerning the nature of these processes and when they occur is given in a number of other sources and need not detain us here. Differentiation and generalization themselves have many subcategories that Foa and Foa elaborate.

The process whereby differentiation and generalization emerge as early structures includes communication among individuals, who exchange both information and other resources. The center of the system revolves around the processes and contexts whereby these resources are exchanged. All objects and processes that serve as communicative issues for people are classified into six categories: love, status, information, money, goods, and services. Another key concept within the system is the idea, already discussed above, of role. The exchange of resources is largely accomplished during the process of socialization and later by individuals filling the conditions demanded of one societal role or the other. Thus the theory takes on the task of describing a large variety of generalized conditions by which individuals exchange six types of resources. We shall pursue some of the major considerations within that framework in order to extract the major epistemological characteristics of the theory.

Clearly, an individual must learn to differentiate among the various resources. Differentiation between love and services, linked in the mother by the child, needs to have the previous perception developed that there is a difference between self and others as actors. The initial nondifferentiation between services and love, Foa and Foa take as the basis of the very strong attachment between infant and mother, a point emphasized by Freud in a somewhat different manner. Differentiation between status and love requires the acquisition of language, since most activities connected with status are verbal. This being the case, the structures found in language themselves enter the system as subsidiary to a total conception of human activity. The authors provide a pyramidal model for the differentiation of the six resources from an initial undifferentiated state and discuss empirical evidence to support this scheme. Since resources are related, the distance between some (services and love) are less than between others (information and love). Thus, from an initial undifferentiated stage, services and love are discriminated into goods and services and goods eventually into goods and money. Love is differentiated into love and status and status into status and information.

The exchange of the various resources eventually yields familial and societal norms regarding the behavior of a child and its mother or mother surrogate, or regarding the behavior of any dyadic relationship. What should the child do, what would mother want the child to do, what should mother do; are all questions that are resolved by the mother's acceptance or rejection, following a particular choice on the part of the growing child. From this sequence of reinforcement, the idea of ideal behavior arises. The differentiation between self and others as actors is crucial in the differentiation between actual and ideal.

This and similar activities results in the development of cognitive classes of social events. These various classes are formed into configurations and involve a combination of actor's viewpoint and level (actual versus ideal). One of the general principles running through the organization of these classes is that variables more similar in conceptual context will be more related empirically. This is an interesting reversal of a common behavioristic idea that variables related empirically (that is, accidently) will yield verbal behavior (cognition), which relates the variables in thought. Thus Foa and Foa's theory distinctly includes the process of functional reinforcement among a variety of behavioral and perceptual elements. However, it does not sacrifice the idea that a cognitive element has characteristics of its own not reducible to the empirical components of reinforcement, even though the cognitive class initially might have been formed through some process of reinforcement. The system concentrates upon developmental sequences that interact with one another and yield the social characteristics typical of human beings. Once these structures have been designated, presumably accurate descriptions of social situations can be built, which will allow for specific predictions. Relationships among resource classes in terms of their influence on human behavior is a major feature of the system. Based on certain empirical research, Foa and Foa have attempted to indicate the relationship among these resource classes.

The conditions under which a resource is exchanged are produced by a need developing in an individual for maintaining a resource within a comfortable range. When the amount of resource falls below the lower level of the range, an individual is said to have a need for this particular resource and will be motivated to increase it. When the amount of resource exceeds the upper limit, an individual will be motivated to reduce the amount of resource through the exchange behavior. The accumulation of resources beyond maxima allows the individual power in that class. Here the Foas introduce a revision of the notion of homeostasis. The modern interpretation of this concept includes attention to the upper limits of the needed substance. The older form attended only to the lower limit of need (for example, Clark Hull and the concept of drive reduction). Thus the motivational conceptualization for the Foa and Foa theory is of the balance variety. The optimum ranges for the six resources varies among them: the optimal range of money varies from 0 to infinity and the optimal range of love is the smallest of the six. The system then deals with the exchange of resources presenting a great deal of relevant experimental work.

As Foa and Foa have pointed out, human beings have a need for the exchange of resources, while the nature of cognitive structure sets the rules for the way these exchanges will be made. These structures are seen to be invariant across cultures.

The epistemological core of the system centers on the processes of the exchange of resources. The success or failure of the system thus revolves around the ability to conceptualize a human social interaction as principally an exchange of these resources. There is no question that people exchange love, goods, services, money, status, and information. The derivative question is whether or not focus upon this exchange is best in explaining social interaction.

Since the Foas' system utilizes a motivational model based on optimum supply of a given resource, it suffers from the limitations of that approach. The major difficulty with motivational models is that they exclude the idea of intrinsic interest as a reason for organismic action. Since the six resources include more phenomena than most formal motivational systems, the generality of this system is greater. However, interest in doing something for its own sake, for example, having a pleasant, ritualistic, but noninformative conversation with someone, may clearly not involve the exchange of love, status, services, goods, information, or money. The motivational theories based on a balance model of intake and output weaken when they attempt to generalize to areas that seem goalless as, for example, play. Play does not seem to be an exchange of any of the resources listed by the Foas.

Aside from this limitation, the theory is one of the very few that has attempted to fuse objective, in this case, reinforcement explanation with cognitive structural explanation and has indicated at which levels these different epistemological approaches are best applied to various kinds of social interaction.

8

Developmental Theory

Cognitive and socioemotional development beginning at birth and continuing to adulthood are processes that are highly relevant to most psychological theories. Psychoanalytic theories of whatever persuasion identify early development as an important determiner of later adult behavior. Any dynamic structural theory also requires description of the cognitive and emotional development of the organism from birth since any given structure is produced by genetic disposition in interaction with previous experience. Functional input–output types of theories, however, do not require such a developmental focus. In short, any theory with a structural reference, including psychoanalysis, requires some attention to early human development. One might also argue that the biologically prior problem of psychology is to understand infancy. Jean Piaget has constructed the current most significant and compelling system of cognitive development.

A good part of Piaget's (1971b) conception of structuralism depends upon the mathematical model that derives from group theory and, more particularly, from Gödel's (Nagel & Newman, 1958) conception of the power of the axiomatic method. Gödel's work also provided a conceptual foundation for the general nature of psychological theory by delineating the limitations and possibilities of its structure. He proved that it is impossible to establish the internal logical consistency of a very large class of deductive systems, particularly elementary arithmetic, unless one adopts principles of reasoning so complex that their own internal consistency is as open to doubt as the systems themselves.

Through an ingenious system of numbering, Gödel showed that an arithmetical formula G that represents the meta-mathematical statement, "the formula G is not demonstrable," could be constructed. He also showed that G is demonstrable if and only if its formal negation *not* G is demonstrable. If a

130

formula and its negation are both formally demonstrable, the arithmetical calculus in which they are imbedded is not consistent. If the calculus is consistent, neither G nor *not* G is formally derivable from the axioms of arithmetic. Therefore, if arithmetic is consistent, G is a formally undecidable formula. Gödel also proved that, although G is not formally demonstrable, it nevertheless is a true arithmetical formula. Hence, since G is both true and formally undecidable, the axioms of arithmetic are incomplete. That is, we cannot deduce all arithmetical truth from the axioms of arithmetic.

Gödel also established that arithmetic is *essentially* incomplete because even if additional axioms were assumed, so that the true formula G could be formally derived from the augmented set of axioms, another true but formally undecidable formula could be constructed.

Gödel next described how to construct an arithmetical formula A that represents the meta-mathematical statement, "arithmetic is consistent," and he proved that the formula *if A then G* is formally demonstrable. Finally, he showed that formula A is not demonstrable. From this it follows that the consistency of arithmetic cannot be established by reasoning that can be represented in the formal arithmetical calculus.

It is clear (Lana, 1969a) that all inferential psychological scientific systems must involve deduction. Therefore, Gödel's proof is of value in understanding the nature of theorizing in psychology. It is not possible to make an induction within any *theory* without deduction being involved from a set of implicit or explicit basic principles that are axiomatic in character. This follows since certain axioms of method are assumed in the very process of inference itself (Lana, 1969a), particularly as it involves the conception of causation.

Gödel's proof does not exclude meta-mathematical proof of the consistency of arithmetic; it simply means that this proof cannot be mirrored by the formal deductions of arithmetic. It is also true that the proof or demonstration of the validity of the structure of a scientific system (its form, not content) cannot be demonstrated by terms contained within that system itself. Reference to terms outside both the formal and empirical framework of that system must be invoked to accomplish that task, as, for example, when certain principles of logic are used to demonstrate the validity of a conclusion made within the framework of a predictive system.

Appropos of this point is Nagel's and Newman's (1958) suggestion that the brain itself embodies a structure of rules of operation, which is far more powerful than the structure of currently conceived artificial machines. Thus modeling from computers to brains is inappropriate, although modeling from brains to computers may not be (Chomsky, 1964; Foa & Foa, 1974). Nagel and Newman further suggested that the resources of the human intellect have not been and cannot be formalized, and that new principles of demonstration await further invention and discovery. In short, man's intellective talents or logical systems must *of necessity* be forever in advance of the systems discovered by him to explain his universe and *himself* (Nagel & Newman, 1958).

Piaget was inspired by Gödel's discovery to conceive the idea of psychological structure as a system of transformations similar to those in modern mathematics. The structure of the components of human cognition is constantly building upon previous structures subsumed within it. The limits of formalization of any structure implies that a higher level structure will always need to be found, which will include the preceding one. Piaget indicates that earlier structural forms (for example, those appearing in Gestalt theories of perception) were static and therefore included no dynamic principles. The growth and change of perception cannot be explained simply by forms set down now and forever. These limits to formalization indicate that there is "no 'form as such' or 'content as such,' that each element — from sensory motor acts through operations, to theories — is always simultaneously form to the content it subsumes and content for some higher form."

Structure is composed of three key elements — wholeness, transformation, and self-regulation. Wholeness refers to the fact that the elements of structure are subordinated to laws, and it is in terms of these laws that the structure of the whole system is defined. Laws of wholeness are structuring. It is the constant duality of always being simultaneously structuring and structure that is at the basis of the structuralist idea of law or rule. The concept of the dialectic is similar to the idea of transformation. Transformation thus refers to the dynamic element of change within structure. Structures are also self-regulating in that they entail self-maintenance and closure, the three basic mechanisms of which are rhythm (e.g., biological rhythms), regulation, and operations.

For Piaget explanation requires that there are discernible principles underlying phenomena and that these hypothetical objects or processes actually influence one another. Frequently, the characteristic qualities of such inferred entities resemble our own cognitive operations, and it is to the extent that there is such a correspondence between subjective and objective activities that we feel we understand. Causal explanation requires that the operations used to deal with objects and processes are of the same "reality" class as that of objects and processes themselves. In short, the requirement is that reality be constituted of operators.

We first discover causality in our own intentional sensory–motor action. As children we become aware of the transmission of movement and the sequence of change and resistance. This action is the source of cognitive operations of a similar sort.

Organic structures. From Piaget's argument so far, it is clear that the human organism itself is the paradigmatic structure for all others (including mathematical structures). The organism can easily be conceived as a "systematic whole of self-regulating transformations" (Piaget, 1971, p. 44). Consequently, by a thorough knowledge of the organism we would both understand its complex physical nature and its role as the originator of behavior. We are, unfortunately far from this accomplishment.

Homeostasis is essentially a structural – biological idea. It is possible to conceive of structuralism as a cybernetic loop such that the organism selects its environment while being conditioned by it. The implication is that the notion of structure as a self-regulating system is expanded to include the genetic and typical environmental characteristics of the organism and parent species.

Psychological structures. Piaget has been most interested in the genesis of intelligence. Historically, psychologists have almost always concentrated upon already formed adult intelligence, such as the Würzberg school, which failed to examine the biological and psychogenetic roots of thought.

The construction of cognitive structures yields the concept of necessity, which has classically been thought to be the initial assumption rather than the product of learning. It takes about 12 years before logical structures are fully elaborated. Through the interaction of reflective abstraction, which furnishes increasingly complex materials for construction, and equilibration mechanisms, which yield structures with internal reversibility, the concept of necessity is produced. The child eventually develops understanding of concepts like function and identity. They constitute structures in the sense of categories. Numbers are constructed by synthesizing seriation and inclusion, and measurement is constructed by synthesizing partition and order relations. Magnitude, previously understood only in the ordinal sense, becomes cardinal, and the conservation principles, which earlier were lacking, are now established. Hence, structures are formed out of operations. Piaget's understanding of these structures is descriptive in that he observed the genesis of these forms of thinking in the child without necessarily attaching these activities to causal mechanisms of any sort. However, the developed structure becomes the basis for the next higher, or more complex, level of activity. The child is able to take some of these activities, such as seriation, and combine them with others based on already existing characteristics of thought. Logical structures are neither absolutely given in the genetic possibilities of the organism nor are they freely learned or invented. Instead, construction is constantly regulated by equilibration requirements. What is true and seemingly absolute in an organism can be best understood as being a dynamic part of organic life rather than as some given static essence in the old Platonic sense. The quality that underlies physical reality is constantly in a process of construction rather than a set of completed structures.

In addition to the development of basic categories of thought, the acquisition of language, in general, presupposes the prior formation of sensory – motor intelligence. This supports Chomsky's notion that there is, necessarily, a prelinguistic substratum to rational thought. However, intelligence antedating speech is not apparent in early childhood. The gradual coordination of assimilation schemes and the processes of repetition, ordering and associative connecting yield the coordination of sensory–motor schemata, which, as we have seen, are active participants in the formation of cognitive forms. Thus, language is not the source of logic, but is grounded in it.

Social analysis and structure.   Older forms of social structure usually contained the idea of "emergence" as the unexplained dynamic that produced the group structure from its component parts. The new form seeks the laws of composition of social structures. The idea is to derive or predict empirical systems from the postulation of deep structures that underlies social behavior. This search for deep structure minimizes the common psychological emphasis in many objective theories on some form of associationism. Indeed, certain deep structures and their derivatives (such as the logic of oppositions and correlations, exclusions and inclusions, compatibles and incompatibles (à la Lévi-Strauss) explain the laws of association and not vice versa. Again, we may emphasize that thought structures are prior to the social order.

Social structures are comparable to mathematical categories, that is, as sets of objects and their possible mutual applications.

Structure and subject.   Piaget's understanding of thought can be said to be an attempt to discover the development of cognitive structures of which the individual is unaware except by special reflection. There is an epistemological parallel to the Freudian idea that conscious emotional life is influenced by unconscious factors of which the individual is not aware except on similar special reflection.

Piaget has sought to make sense of the "intelligence of intelligent behavior." How is it that people can solve problems when the origins of lines of solution coming from an individual are a mystery to them? An art of intelligence does not contain, within one's consciousness of it, the mechanisms of the intelligence itself. Explanation can only be in terms of structures such as groups, networks, semigroups, and so on. This view of cognition forces a salutory separation between the epistemic subject and the individual existential subject. Is the dichotomy any more productive than several that we have already rejected? At this point in time, I believe so. As we have seen, an examination of any problem seems to require polarities, and hence a dialectic, in the process of solution.

The epistemic subject possesses a cognitive nucleus, which is the commonality of all subjects at the same age. These considerations yield a conception of subject that is a true synthesis of the idea of the purely private individual and the necessity to search for abstraction that all science and philosophy must acknowledge. The quality of becoming, so characteristic of subject (see Chapter 6), is preserved in the coming to be of structures through their constant transformations. They are *under construction.* Piaget indicated that even biological structures can be viewed as evolving products or as static and given for all time by the original DNA molecule.

EXTENSION OF PIAGET'S EPISTEMOLOGY

A consideration of consistency and completeness as they are related to one another within the framework of Gödel's proof can be used, at least by analogy, to reveal certain interesting characteristics of major psychological theories. Even though Skinner has long denied that his system is a theory at all but rather a method, it is clear that there are definite theoretical implications in his work. It is therefore possible to examine this system in the light of the Gödelian discoveries.

The operations used to activate Skinner's system involve the manipulation of variables so as to produce various reinforcements that accompany, closely in time, certain behaviors. This linkage is what has been described as operant conditioning. Through these various manipulations, Skinner has been able to develop relatively simple functions that describe input to, and output from, an organism in a reinforcement situation. The conclusions or products of the system are these mathematical functions.

Let us assume for a moment that all possible reinforcement functions have been established. If this were the case, Skinner's system would be complete in a mathematical sense. However, if the system can be shown to be derivable from a set of premises external to its reinforcement qualities, then it follows that the system is incomplete. In *Assumptions of Social Psychology* (Lana, 1969a) I believe I demonstrated that Skinner's system both is derivable from principles outside of it and does not successfully explain phenomena that it purports to. That is, the acquisition and use of language, because of limitations imposed on it by its structure, cannot solely or even principally be explained (including developing successful predictions) by *any* reinforcement system.

Gestalt psychology is a system somewhat in contrast to Skinner's. Again reasoning by analogy, the system seems to be complete but inconsistent. The complete quality of this system can be seen on an examination of the principles of Gestalt psychology by Kurt Koffka (1935). Premises and assumptions concerning the nature of geometrical forms and of innate responses to those forms by human beings structure the assumptive core of the system. From these premises is drawn a description of perceptual phenomena. An epistemological focus is constantly in evidence such that there is an attempt to examine every assumption that the system makes.

Of course, Koffka and other early Gestalters could have failed at this task; however, let us assume that all possible premises have been examined that are implied by the Gestalt theory of perception and have been found to be exhaustive. Having accomplished this, one finds that the method of Gestalt psychology, which is essentially descriptive, disallows for convincing empirical demonstration of the various predictions of the system. In short, Gestalt psychology's weakness of method is inconsistent with the richness of its theory, whereas Skinner's system is weak in theory and rich in method. Both of these positions have often been taken as antagonistic and this antagonism has been central to the history of modern psychology. Why is this the case? The admission of Skinnerian behaviorism as method rather than theory coupled with the observation that Gestalt theory is weak in method, clearly indicates that one system cannot give way to the other in order to produce a more complete explanation of human phenomena. The insistence by the adherents of either system that theirs is the most fruitful general approach to understanding all of human behavior is clearly doomed to failure not only because there has been insufficient time to develop each system but, perhaps more keenly, because both are virtual transformations in an evolving picture of the structure of human existence. We shall speak more of this evolution in the final chapter of this book.

STRUCTURE AND PHENOMENOLOGY

It is possible to gain a good deal of insight into the theoretical possibilities for psychology by examining the epistemological basis of Piaget's structuralism in comparison with the development of phenomenology (Piaget, 1971a, 1972). There is a sense in which the two positions cross and indicate in a rather subtle manner each other's limits. Piaget dealt with the presumed exclusivity of the phenomenological position from science and rejected this conclusion. He also argued against the possibility that science emerges from phenomenological attention to immediate experience. We have seen in Chapter 3 that one of the key assumptions of Husserl and other phenomenologists was that the epistemological tenets of science are subsequent to principles of phenomenological inquiry. Should this not be the case, the universality of phenomenology as method is considerably weakened. This, however, would not disturb the idea that the scientific enterprise *generally* is yielded by immediate experience — indeed, this observation is a truism.

Piaget noted that philosophy has always seen itself as either logically, epistemologically, or metaphysically prior to the enterprise of science or art. Piaget challenged this position and raised the question as to whether or not there is any valid philosophy beyond that of a philosophy of science. He did, however, conclude that ethics is a legitimate separate nonscientific philosophical enterprise. Piaget observed that work in phenomenology, including the simple writing of a novel that is a descriptive passage of real life events, requires an epistemology. Indeed, anyone who writes as a systematist, even via description, is forced into an epistemology. This epistemology must be an abstract knowledge system as are all others. Its characteristics may be different from those associated with experimental science—it may attempt to stay closer to immediate experience—but it is already conceptual if any order is sought.

The phenomenologists made the mistake of looking for an absolute beginning to perception in immediate experience and assume that we can know what is most important about perception from this absolute beginning. There is no absolute beginning in immediate experience because there is virtually no absolute beginning to existence that we can know about. Even assuming that existence begins absolutely at birth, whatever one is experiencing is in part connected with his own actions that have been conditioned by earlier activity.

One of the difficulties with phenomenology is the implicit assumption that what went on before a given experience is of little consequence. However, if developmental psychology is meaningful at all, what went before a given experience is extremely important. Indeed the whole idea of developmental psychology, which explicitly indicates that in order to understand an individual at any point in his life it is necessary to understand the sequence from birth onward, rests in a somewhat contradictory juxtaposition to phenomenology. Phenomenology, as we have suggested, cries out for a developmental psychology, in that the emphasis on immediate experience assumes a set of capabilities at a certain time in a person's life that in turn, must be understood by prior developmental sequences. If, in the development of thought in childhood, one observes that there are ways of thinking that appear at certain ages and not before, then the idea of a developmental cognitive sequence with its related actions is demonstrated and is directly related to phenomenological inquiry.

It is relatively simple to demonstrate that the mental operations of the child change sequentially and are highly predictable, in part from the child's exposure to the environment and in part because of the developing capabilities of the central nervous system. Phenomenology and all philosophies are systems of understanding adults. There is no real philosophical epistemology of childhood. Hence, it is appropriate that Piaget be the first to introduce a genetic epistemology that by its nature represents a restriction on the positions of Husserl and Merleau-Ponty.

Since immediate experience, on which phenomenology is based, is direct perception of what is true for the individual and since science is presumably derived from immediate experience, science should then be an abstraction of what is immediately perceivable. In reality, science works the other way around. Science tells you that something is different from what you suspected. The activity of science requires abstraction from precedents and finding things different from what is immediately apparent. It, therefore, cannot be based on immediate experience in the way that Husserl has suggested. For example, the immediate experience of an individual yields the conclusion that the earth stands still while the sun moves around it. Science tells us that something very different is occurring in reality, from what we are apparently experiencing.

A conclusion one can draw from this point is that science and phenomenology are not really attempting to deal with the same issues or are not dealing with an understanding of human existence from the same perspective or level. It also seems to give the lie to the idea that science emanates from phenomenology in other than a very general way since dealing directly with immediate experience seems counter to what science typically does, namely, dig beneath a one-to-one correlation between experience and its description in order to determine a higher level abstraction relevant to the experience.

Piaget concluded that one cannot look for the beginnings of science in perception because perception yields only the realities of immediate experience. This is a critical point, for it runs counter to what we have seen in the initial chapter as being not only the chronological but the conceptual beginning of psychology. The idea that psychology begins with perception as the process whereby the world comes to the individual and the individual to the world is an idea that yielded both British empiricism and Kantianism, and thereby behaviorism and phenomenology. Science comes from the world of action. This world obviously includes perception but also includes that which is abstracted from perception, namely, motor activity, cognition, and emotion. This implies an indissoluable fusion of perception with native proclivities in the organism and with the world as it is to the individual who exists within it and who creates it. This description would not be acceptable to a phenomenologist.

Although Husserl and Merleau-Ponty admitted that the integration called for is implied in action, according to them, abstraction is not removable from immediate experience, even though Merleau-Ponty has indicated that abstraction itself is a form of immediate experience. For Piaget, however, the processes of abstraction are fused with immediate experience to produce cognitive or motor action. Abstract thought corrects immediate experience and, therefore, action as it develops. The phenomenologists are guilty of creating a meaningless epistemological dichotomy, something they accuse the empiricists and traditional philosophers of, by virtue of their separation of abstraction from immediate experience, which does not take account of the possibility of constant and inevitable interaction between them. Piaget's point is that abstraction is not derivable from immediate experience; it is not even separable from it in the first place.

Through the process of eidetic reduction, which we have already described, Husserl hoped to come to what he called a series of transcendental essences that are the elements of these reductions. The process implies that one comes to a series of reductions through the phenomenological technique that then represents something that could not have been arrived at by either the traditional abstracted means of science or by traditional philosophy. Piaget suggested that in coming to these conclusions via eidetic reduction, it is necessary to use processes that are not implied in Husserl's explanation.

Husserl believed he had discovered the possibility for pure or transcendental intuitions or reductions. He believed he had discovered the way to make immediate perceptual conclusions regarding immediate experience. At the same time, he hoped to open the way to autonomous philosophical knowledge freed from the empirical subject and from science connected with it. Husserl's fundamental mistake lay in the fact that his transcendental subject's pure intuition is still an activity of a subject in which the object or essence admittedly enters, but where conclusion drawing requires an epistemic subject. Any explanation that requires a process other than a simple one-to-one description of an event (and perhaps even that) always involves the process of abstraction. Therefore, an intuition is still a psychologism—arguing from fact to norm.

Piaget contended that one always has the subject as subject in whatever he may be doing and that he is capable of scientific inquiry. The method that yields scientific insight is itself a norm and this, in turn, is psychological insight. The principal criticism of phenomenological method is that whatever phenomenologists do in their analyses, by their very examination of immediate experience they are proceeding ostensibly in the same way as science. To say that the intuition is pure presupposes a normative justification. That is, the justification arises from a process of inquiry not given by the intuition itself.

The intuition itself has to do with the way one sees something, but not with the way one concludes that it is true. Cavaille (Piaget, 1972) has stated, "either logic is dependent upon the intuition of the transcendental subject and is no longer absolute or it is absolute and no longer requires a transcendental intuition [p. 105]." The counter argument is that transcendental intuition is necessary in order to see this absolute. I believe it is clearer to conclude that the functions of logic are absolute at the level at which we use them. A platonist would indicate that there are ideas, which one either has or does not have, that are nonetheless absolute, but that it may take some effort to come to them. This is not inconsistent with the conclusions just drawn. So far as illustrating the existence of an absolute in the phenomenal sense used here, it is sufficient to point out that we act and believe that the principles of mathematics are absolute.

We have seen that Piaget did not reject the notion of a phenomenological reduction but did reject the idea that this process is different from the activity of science. Piaget consistently objected to the idea that the methods of phenomenology are different from any methods found within science or indeed within traditional logic or epistemology. He also objected to the phenomenological contention that the subject matter of phenomenology, immediate experience, is not also the subject matter of science. He concluded that immediate experience can be examined by utilizing methods that always include abstraction and that, therefore, overlap the methods of science and mathematics. He would agree that certain narrow conceptions of science have excluded phenomenological reduction and consequently an examination of immediate experience. However, this methodology is not necessary for science and logic.

Piaget shared the observation that it is important to deal with the various levels of activity in the subject. It is clear that a subject is an individual with his own immediate experience and that at any time be can change and become an epistemological one. An individual becomes an epistemological subject through the development of the coordination of his thought, which eventually brings him to utilize logical necessity rather than empirical verification in drawing certain conclusions. This process is somewhat similar to Husserl's phenomenological reduction. A child initially relates to the world in a way that empirically verifies it for him. He operates as a conditioned object. When he learns a variety of abstractions, he no longer depends on empirical verification to deal with the world, but broadens his epistemic possibilities by being able to utilize logical necessity. At a certain age the child thus becomes capable of a phenomenological reduction. He is capable of directly perceiving, acting, and living in the world. Hence, by the natural process of growing and changing, both physiologically and in terms of reaction to his own immediate experience, the child develops the forms of action and thought which characterize the thought of the scientist. This analysis is beyond any sort of positivism and is at the heart of a phenomenology that Piaget could accept. Thus, if human beings develop the possibility for abstraction and hence phenomenal reduction through a series of stages in childhood, this constitutes a confirmation of certain aspects of phenomenology.

We have seen, however, that the phenomenology of Husserl and Merleau-Ponty is a phenomenology of adults. They have assumed normal adult age, intelligence, development, and experience and have built a phenomenal reduction from that level. It has been suggested that phenomenologists see science as derivative from phenomenal activity because the phenomenal methods used seem to be immediately given in the subject who is always an adult. Were they to examine the immediate experience of children they would find a different situation. Certain ways of dealing with the world are absent at one age and present at another. There is nothing counter to science in finding that physiological development is correlated with ways of living in the world, although this is counter to positivism. Hence the observation of repeatable facts and conclusions yielding norms is absolutely necessary if we are to understand anything about human beings.

The result of this "Piagetian phenomenology," which is firmly placed within the concept of modern science, is that his theory of child development is even more deeply imbedded in the concept of structure. Structure is a paradigm for prediction *and* theory since it involves empirical manipulation *and* immediate experience. It fuses phenomenology and science as phenomenology sought to fuse subject and object, but created as a by-product a separation of phenomenological from scientific methods. Since method is the sine qua non of science, the separation was irreparable even though phenomenologists think of science as being yielded by basic phenomenological principles. Thus, even the phenomenologists in their attempt to fuse subject and object have fallen prey to that perhaps perculiarly Western sensibility of constantly analyzing and dichotomizing all aspects of existence. Piaget can be said to have made progress toward fusing subject and object and toward fusing phenomenal method with science.

STRUCTURE AND MATHEMATICS

It has long been a puzzle as to how abstract mathematics so often fits the determinations of the physical world. Mathematics is highly abstract and is clearly not learned from direct experience in the sense that its characteristics are observable in the objects and processes in the world, yet it "fits" empirical processes so well in theory development.

Piaget attempted to solve the puzzle. Through mathematics a subject may structure his world. Mathematics is not abstractable from empirical observation. This in turn suggests that genetic structure allows for the forms of mathematical logic that have evolved for the subject in his interaction with the world. Structure in mathematics is akin to structure in biology. We have seen that Piaget has taken models from mathematical structure and applied them to developmental sequences. To the extent that they are useful as explanatory and predictive devices one is able to understand both the structure of human cognitive development and the structure of mathematics itself. The systems are intertwined so that successful extension in either area spreads inferentially to the other. Hence, there is no knowledge system that is separate from any other. Among others, there is the implication that philosophies of whatever type cannot be separated from science. Over the years theorists have paid lip service to this fusion of knowledge, but have theorized as if there were distant and separate possibilities for understanding. Along certain minor theoretical dimensions, it is possible to separate out certain methodological approaches, but the most comprehensive questions asked about human beings must be dealt with by a multileveled intuitive approach. If psychology is even slightly more broad in its explanatory possibilities than various empiricisms would imply, there is absolutely no break between traditional philosophy and psychology.

Clearly psychology in particular and science in general must be able to deal with the kinds of problems Piaget poses. Verbal learning is not all there is to cognition. Sensation is not perception. There is no possibility that knowledge of the physiology of sensation will totally explain seeing because the modalities of understanding are different. Objective and subjective qualities are at work and must be experienced by means of a fusion of methods suggested more by Piaget's structuralism then by a simple combination of academically traditional areas of science. The process of genetic development requires obvious physical and physiological changes, which in turn requires the scientist to attend to the operation of the central nervous system.

Analysis of the central nervous system and physiology in general is a different epistemological enterprise from an analysis of experience, although the two sets of data may parallel each other closely. For example, if one discovers that a child begins to understand reversibility between certain ages and at the same time the cortex fires in a certain structural pattern at a given rate, the two classes of information may be related, but *complete* information about one cannot replace the other body of information without loss of meaning. This implies that a short-circuiting process is possible, but not direct prediction of cognitive events by physiological means. By electrical or other means one may adjust the firing of the cells of the cortex and thereby change a behavioral or cognitive event, but not produce a specific meaning or thought. Direction is not possible because the entities of understanding are not separate in the first place. It is not possible to separate an understanding of brain structure from the method used to discriminate brain structure from thought. Both physiological and cognitive analysis participates in the same higher level epistemological structure, which is holistic in character and thus disallows reduction of either analysis to the other yet links them inexorably. It then follows that structure is an active principle in the conceptual understanding of behavioral, experiential, and physiological modalities.

9

Physiological Theory

Of all the disciplines of psychology, physiological inquiry seems to be the one most associated with the methodologies and theoretical schema that have been so successful in other areas of science. It is an area that has enjoyed some of the successes of chemistry and biology. Indeed, in the past 20 years, many interesting discoveries have been made in the realm of physiological psychology.

The major development in physiological psychology over the past several years has been the further delineation of centers of behavioral control in the central nervous system. This development is the continuation of a long-term interest in brain localization. Several years ago work was begun on brain implantation. It consisted of an electrochemical analysis of reactions to stimulation of certain brain structures. This work has shown that certain emotional reactions are directly controlled by cell aggregates in the central brain portion. Perhaps the most dramatic discovery has been the delineation of many of the functions of the hypothalamus and the limbic systems. Advances were made in analyzing these structures by the construction of sterotaxic equipment, which allowed for implantations of very fine electrodes so that a particular center could be stimulated. These techniques and equipment have recently been refined to an even greater degree.

It is fairly certain that a peer system exists in the central core of the brain that consists of two levels, the lower in the hypothalamus and the higher in the limbic system, specifically within the amygdala.

Electrochemical stimulation of certain points in the hypothalamus provides a fear reaction without any signs of pain in a stimulated animal. When the cat is used as an experimental subject, its pupils actually dilate, heart rate is increased, and there is great restlessness and attempts to escape the apparatus, or else the animal may completely freeze. Stimulation of certain parts of the

143

amygdala produces similar responses. Stimulation of corresponding fields in both areas produces a decrease in fearfulness. When the amygdala is removed, cats and rats exhibit no fear of their natural enemies such as snakes and man. The counterbalancing systems of relief that eliminate fear are confounded with anger reactions. Since fear and anger are inextricably connected, the hypothalamus and limbic system are in control of both. With the stimulations of portions of both systems, animals can be made behaviorally tame or ferocious. However, evidence for the existence of a reciprocal center for anger is more convincing than that for a reciprocal center for fear (Lana & Rosnow, 1972).

These recent developments in physiological psychology are conceptually continuous with physiological thinking initiated a few hundred years ago. The central idea of phrenology was that the brain, which was structurally convoluted and had identifiable lobes and fissures, might best be studied in terms of the linkage among these various substructures and their potentially different functions. Once the brain had been established as the human control center, the next step was obvious. The initial phrenological approach simply examined the external contours of the skull and attempted to correlate extended portions of it with various kinds of behavior.

The basic phrenological idea is essentially similar to the more exact and useful conception of today. It was only a matter of time before methodological advances allowed scientists to begin the correlation of internal brain parts with their behavioral function. Eventually people like Florens and Broca discovered various brain centers corresponding to functions such as hearing and seeing.

The earliest methods for correlating behavior with brain area were crude. Patients with accidental lesions in determinable portions of the brain were examined for behavioral or cognitive dysfunction. This was a haphazard affair and it was never certain that the damage existed only in the brain portion under examination. The other technique was to insult surgically a specific portion of the brain in either animals or human beings. Control was improved with this technique, but was still far from accurate. As suggested earlier, it was only when techniques were developed for stimulating certain select small portions of the brain while minimizing the amount of extraneous damage, that advances in correlating brain portion with behavior could be made. Larger brain parts such as the frontal cortex and cerebellum remained areas more likely to be examined by the older techniques. Sterotaxic and other related techniques have allowed the correlation of certain brain parts with manifestations of emotion and drive so that functions such as eating, drinking, fear, and anger have been identified with specific brain centers. A great deal is known about how these centers function. What typically has not been touched by these techniques are thought processes such as abstraction and reason.

The development of research on brain physiology from phrenology to current predications about the nature of the hypothalamus and other lower brain centers is highly useful in localizing areas in control of particularly important human behavior. However impressive these discoveries, they lack a certain specificity because of the character of the central nervous system. The difficulty in identifying particular functions in, for example, the hypothalamus is that the cells involved in that particular portion that control anger are not necessarily structurally or functionally different from cells in other parts of the brain. The interactive contexts of the various structures in that portion of the hypothalamus that controls anger is much more difficult to analyze compared, for example, with the function of a noncentral body organ. What seems most clear is that particular areas within various parts of the brain are inextricably involved with certain emotions and drives. The brain physiologist or psychologist who would attempt to further delineate the function of the hypothalamus has fundamentally two directions in which to move.

There is first, the ceaseless attempt to reduce the unit examined to its component parts. In this case, discovery of the structure and function of single cells within a certain brain area would be highly appropriate. The goal, of course, is to determine some key within those structures that is able to account for the peculiar functional aspects of the larger brain portion. A discovery of substructures and their attendant functions implies that a further reduction is most likely possible, perhaps to biochemical elements within the cell. The second direction is to concentrate on a more holistic or integrated approach that would attempt to determine various interconnections of the hypothalamus with other brain portions and to discover their relationship to environmental stimuli and specific behavior.

Very recently, a significant reduction has taken place involving the structure and function of the single cell. A great deal of the experimentation on single cells has come from those researchers interested in perception rather than those interested in emotion-related structures such as the hypothalamus or amygdala.

The theoretical implications of single cell analysis will be discussed within the framework of Konorski's theory of brain function.

THEORY IN PHYSIOLOGICAL PSYCHOLOGY

The reliance on the idea that associations of single cells form the physiological basis for behavior has often been accompanied by the position that external stimulation largely controls neuronal firing. With recent intensive work on the single cell, the idea of external stimulation dominating single cell response has been minimized. Generally, theories depending on more complex basic physiological units to explain behavior rely less on external stimulation and more on the nuances and complexities of the brain itself. This is particularly true of intrinsic action tendencies that are either independent of external stimuli or initiated by them, but essentially follow their own course after initiation. We see that theory in physiological psychology bears a distinct similarity to theoretical tendencies in other areas of psychology, and, again, that all theories in the field tend to emphasize either external objective control or subjective intrinsic regulation.

We have seen that interpretations of the nature of the central nervous system began with developments in phrenology that implied that distinct parts of the brain control certain behaviors. This notion developed into the idea of brain localization, which in turn gave way to a neuronal interpretation of central nervous system activity. Edwin G. Boring (1950) has documented the nineteenth and early twentieth century histories of these ideas.

The reflex arc interpretation of neuronal activity suggested a passive substratum of neuron connections stimulated by external processes. Several experiments (Pribram, 1960) over the past few years have indicated that isolated brain tissue shows activity long after initial stimulation has been applied. It has also been shown that there is some spontaneous activity particularly in receptors. The virtually universal acceptance of the idea that brain tissue is active independent of specific stimulation has weakened the s–r reflex arc interpretation as the major principle of neural activity. The idea of a feedback unit has replaced this older idea. The notion that there are loop systems with several mechanical characteristics is more useful than the reflex arc notion as an explanatory device for neuronal activity involving sense receptors. Research has indicated that there are both neuronal aggregates to stimulus inputs and connected neuronal aggregates sensitive to other aggregates. A double feedback system accounts for the obvious interaction between organism and environment in the sense that a stimulus elicits a behavior, which then changes the environment in some way and which, in turn, reinfluences the organism. This implies that there is more activity in the organism to begin with and less external influence than was previously suspected. Intrinsic rhythms within neuronal tissue have been shown through the use of EEG and similar devices.

Once spontaneous activity in the brain was discovered and intrinsic rhythms established, it made conceptual sense to return to a search for specific activities localized in certain brain portions. The cycle of the history of physiological psychology came full tilt with the introduction of the idea of brain localization, its minimization in favor of explanation via stimulus – response reflex arc connections, and the reintroduction of localization with the discovery of spontaneous activity in the brain.

Most research indicates that metabolic and endocrine activity are controlled in various specific portions of the brain. Phenomena such as memory seem to be less localized and are more an activity of the total brain. For example, the reticular formation is associated with specific drives and emotions as well as with general pleasure and pain centers. Modern theories associated with metabolic and endocrine function involve nonhomeostatic interpretations of rhythms that emphasize direction of behavior rather than an arousal–quiescence dimension. Homeostasis has always been a concept associated with an s – r reflex arc concept of brain physiology, since it requires no specific motivational direction, as in eating or drinking, but rather only quiescence or arousal in the total organism. The introduction of the idea of a feedback unit is related to more ambitious attempts to explain brain activity via brain stimulation concepts. Computer and, more generally, communication models have been used recently to present an explanatory context that will include the characteristics most recently discovered about the brain and central nervous system.

Besides brain simulation models, biomodels have also appeared in recent work (Pribram, 1960). The brain is conceived to be an information processing system with a large storage capacity holding complex strategies that may be evoked by specific stimuli. These strategies are presumably determined by the previous experience of the system. One of the weaknesses of this model is that the type and transmission of experience, which form particular storage capacities, are not included in it as theorems or their derivatives. The assimilation of this experience is, of course, susceptible to an attempt at explanation by the same computer modeling, producing a kind of circularity. The success of such an explanation remains problematic.

Information processing systems are of two types — the digital and the analogue. The digital system is akin to the processing of the appearance or nonappearance of a response. The all-or-none interpretation of neuron firing is a digital system. The all-or-none response, over evolutionary time, probably replaced a graded mechanism at the point where an animal became too large not to have a readily available rapid neuronal firing system in order for it to survive. However, neuronal tissue can fire in a graded manner and need not fire to its full potential under given circumstances.

The other computer model system is of the analogue form of which the graded response mechanism is an example. In this system the organism is susceptible to various increments of stimulation to which it can react and feed back to itself further information.

BIOMODELS

There has been some success in showing that memory storage is connected in some way to the synthesis of protein molecules (J. A. Deutsch, 1969). Given a positive relationship, memory storage could be prevented by introducing a substance that inhibits the synthesis of protein. This interpretation suggests that whatever the experiential form of memory, it is correlated with a biological process, namely, the synthesis of protein that takes place in other parts of the body as well as in the brain. Hence, a biochemical process might parallel a cognitive one.

Actually this explanation of memory is part analogue and part correlation of biochemistry with behavior (memory). More direct biomodels have simply taken an intact and complete biological system within the organism, identified its functional components, and applied it to neuronal tissue or general brain function as a model. For example, the mamalian spinal cord exhibits a situation decrement, spontaneous recovery, dishabituation, and sensitization, as well as other responses that are similar to the total organism. Hence, what may be true about the operation of the spinal cord might be taken as a model for the operation of the whole organism. These models have been used in explaining certain learning phenomena. Generally there seems to be little success, however, in the utilization of biomodels. More usually, studies relating physiological entities to learning have used correlational methods to develop theory. That is, during learning the neuronal processes have been examined and recorded in some way. The resulting correlation between these recordings and appropriate behavior, if significant and consistent, has been taken to suggest a causal linkage between the neuronal process and behavior. Correlative work of this sort is important, but the resulting inferences must be made with great caution since a number of interpretations are always possible regarding correlative data.

CORTEX

While brain centers have been discovered that are intimately related to emotions and drives, no such parallel discoveries have been made for cognitive activities such as abstraction, reasoning, and memory. These activities are usually associated with the functions of the cortex; but the evidence that exists for discovering locus of control for drives and emotions in the hypothalamus and medula is not apparent for abstraction, reasoning, and memory. Indeed, it would be surprising if such centers were found. From the early extirpation experiments of Karl Lashley and others, it is evident that cognitive processes involve many portions of the brain and therefore have the status more of integrative rather than of specialized functions.

It is not now possible, and perhaps never will be, to stimulate a certain portion of the cortex to increase reasoning ability or produce a display of abstraction. However, it is an empirical question as to whether the structural and functional aspects of brain physiology can be well enough understood to actually control individual processes of abstraction and reasoning other than by simply removing large parts of the cortex that we know will impair certain aspects of memory.

At least two contemporary scientists have attempted comprehensive theories of central nervous system reaction, particularly that associated with perception. The reception of sense data, its transmission via afferent neurons to the central nervous system, and accompanying behaviors have been the central concern of Jerzi Konorski and J. A. Deutsch. We shall briefly examine these systems and attempt to extract their epistemological bases.

THE SYSTEM OF JERZI KONORSKI

The Polish scientist, Jerzi Konorski (1967), has developed a theory of afferent functioning which, because of the intensive recent work on single cell nerve firing, is of great interest. There are neuronal reference systems that are constructed in the form of a many-layered set of cells. A group of these neurons is called an analyzer. Each analyzer is set in the surface of the body and is connected to more than one complicated arrangement of neurons as one proceeds toward the central nervous system. The final level represents the arrangement of neurons where a message received by a receptive surface is terminated. Each level of this construction is composed of a collection of nerve cells whose axons connect with the next higher level. The axons of the top level are sent outside the given analyzer.

In some of these analyzer systems, each succeeding level has a precise topical arrangement in that one level is a geometric projection of the next level, and so on, down to the first. In some systems, a level is duplicated by a factor of two or three in each succeeding level. The various nerve cells of a particular level of analyzer are connected with the nerve cells of a higher level of analyzer, or the axons are connected with other parts of the nervous system. The first type of cell is called a transit unit. The second type is called an exit unit. Exit units (cells) in the lower levels of each analyzer represent the last connection in the afferent parts of various unconditioned reflex arcs such as the defensive and alimentary reflexes. Exit units at the highest level of an analyzer send axons to the highest levels of other analyzers and form the anatomical substratum of the associative function of the nervous system. Transit units play an intermediary role in elaborating the information within a given axon system. An exit unit plays a role in utilization of this information for various types of behavior. A transit unit has a receptive function and the exit units have a perceptive function. For each unit in a given afferent field of a given analyzer there is a stimulus or a set of stimuli that produces its optimum response in the form of a maximum rate of impulse discharge. These adequate stimuli become more complex the higher the level of the afferent system. The higher systems are formed by the convergence of various units of the lower levels. The unit of the highest level represents the top of a pyramid whose base consists of receptive organs.

Over the years psychologists have noted that although human beings can notice the components of a stimulus configuration, they rarely do so except by a special act of attention. When one is asked to identify a tree he does so by that label, suggesting that he perceives a total configuration rather than the particular edges and curves of the various lines that perceptually compose the trunk, the leaves, and so forth. However, we know that the adequate stimuli for certain lower level unit perceptions are lines, edges, colors, and so on. The question then becomes how to explain not the adequate stimulus for lower level units such as lines and curves but rather the configurational perception. From recent experimental work on single nerve cell activities, particularly Hubel and Wiesel's (1963), it can be concluded that perceptions are represented not by collections of units but by single neurons in the highest level of a particular analyzer. These single units in the highest levels of the analyzers Konorski calls gnostic areas. The units responsible for the particular perceptions he calls gnostic units or gnostic cells. There is a different role played by gnostic areas than that played by transit areas. Transit units, it is recalled, consist of integrations of elements of stimulus receptions to normal complex patterns and constitute the raw material for the gnostic cell or unit. This latter unit represents the biologically meaningful stimulus patterns that are used in associative processes and behavior of the organism.

The formation of gnostic units. Experiments by Hubel and Wiesel (1963) indicate that the projective visual area displays functions that are innate. However, gnostic units are, in part, formed by experience and hence are the result of some type of learning process occurring in conjunction with the structural characteristics of the central nervous system. Physiologically, according to Konorski (1967), learning consists in "transformation of *potential* connections established in ontogeny between two groups of neurons into *actual* connections [p. 86]." Probably an increase in the transmissibility of synaptic contacts linking the axon terminals of the first group with perikaryons of the second group of neurons is the manner in which connection occurs and becomes semipermanent. The result is that in a young organism each presentation of a new stimulus pattern leads to the formation of a larger set of gnostic units than in an older organism.

It is important to note that the Hubel and Wiesel experiments indicated that single nerve units (cells) can perform functions that were previously believed to be performed by aggregations of cells. However, there is no particular data from the Hubel and Wiesel experiments that would indicate that any given cell within an analyzer does the job of a gnostic cell rather than of a transit cell. This is Konorski's extension, not from the physiological data presented by Hubel and Wiesel, but in order to account for the obvious behavioral differences that exist in various types of human and animal perception. We shall return to this point later. Konorski admits that there is no direct evidence for perceptual representations in the cells of the gnostic areas. However, he does suggest that there is a bulk of indirect evidence that comes from neural, anatomical, neural pathological, and psychological considerations. The psychological evidence given is of the nature of the configurational or Gestalt perceptual behavior that was mentioned above; i.e., the organism has a tendency to see wholes and total patterns, which presumably requires a neuronal substructure that precedes, and, in part, is isomorphic to, this perceptual behavior. It is clear that human beings can have unitary holistic perceptions. It is equally clear that there are neuronal and central nervous system arrangements that are correlated with this behavior. Consequently, Konorski's psychological evidence is really no evidence at all other than pointing out what is self-evident. Were individuals not capable of this type of perceptual behavior then one might argue that the gnostic unit does not exist as Konorski suggests, but rather that the neuronal arrangements support part-perceptions of the types seen in various stimulus – response connections of which animals and humans are capable.

Neurological evidence at least indicates differences between the structure of the projective area of the cerebral cortex and the associative areas. The projective areas send their axons only to adjacent areas, which are still part of the same analyzer. Associative areas send their axons to various parts of the cortex through the long associative pathways. Konorski assumes that the highest area levels of the particular analyzers, and therefore the gnostic units, are situated in these areas. This, of course, constitutes a legitimate assumption that at least supports the idea of different function in the associative areas compared with the projective areas. Also, there is evidence that humans with accidental lesions in the projective transit areas of the cortex behave considerably different from those with lesions in areas of the cortex where damage is presumably to the gnostic units.

THE NEURAL PHYSIOLOGICAL SYSTEM
OF J. A. DEUTSCH

Basically the carrier process that communicates both external and internal environmental conditions to parts of the central nervous system is believed to be a fluid that surrounds a set of structures in various places in the central nervous system (J. A. Deutsch, 1969). It is further postulated that there are different elements, each sensitive to different states of the fluid surrounding it, that are related to the various activities of the organism, such as hunger, thirst, and mating. When the central structures are excited they indirectly excite the portion of the motor system that causes the animal to perform a certain persistent type of activity. In time, this activity produces a particular receptor (analyzer) discharge. The discharge from the analyzer is transmitted back to the central structure, which then depresses its excitability to the particular state that excites it. Deutsch depends on a notion that has some empirical support—that conditions in the blood are influential in exciting various structures in the central nervous system. Deutsch summarized his proposition in five postulates: (1) the primary link is set into activity by a feature of the internal environment; (2) when the primary link is active, it indirectly activates the motor organization; (3) the activity in the motor organization causes the environment to vary;

(4) a particular variation of the environment activates the analyzer; (5) the activated analyzer switches off the link. An analyzer is a receptoral system. A motor organization is an effector. Deutsch then attempted to explain, from these basic notions and derivatives, much of the basic behavioral data of psychology such as emotions, curiosity, exploration, reward, reinforcement, insight, and reasoning.

It is clear that although there are differences in the particular emphasis placed on the influence of substances in the blood or on the properties of single cells, the epistemological character of Konorski's and Deutsch's systems are similar. Both focus on reduced central nervous system structure (the single neuron or substances within the blood). This is consistent with the successful inclination of scientists to attempt to reduce any unit of immediate observation to its component parts and study them. Consequently, examination of the function of structures within the cell and within the blood is a natural consequence of the ability to locate them in the first place.

To reiterate, the crucial point for psychologists is that these systems yield the kind of data that is correlative to cognitive and perceptual functions. Unless it is possible to reproduce a specific thought or cognitive category or a specific perception or perceptual category via direct brain short circuiting or manipulation, the data remain, however important, indirect. Remember that it *is* possible to stimulate a certain part of the hypothalamus and create rage or fear in an animal or human being. It has not yet been shown that appropriate types of responses can be directly manipulated by interfering with the processes of the cortex with the exception, already noted, of changes in memory as a result of major lesions in, or extirpation of parts of the cortex.

In conclusion, it can be said that the simple connective interpretations of nervous system firing are inadequate, and indeed theories have moved more in the direction of models of explanation that are closer to the holistic concepts once prevalent in several areas of psychology.

10

Values and Psychology

Although there is no doubt about the success of science in gaining information about physiological and biological topics, the speed of accumulation slows considerably when one is confronted with psychological issues. The reason for this deceleration is partly due to the confounding that results when the machine examines itself. Scientists must turn the very processes they are studying on themselves. The result is artifact in experiment and starkness in theory, both of which produce meaningless conclusions. Part of this difficulty is that structural and/or personal values are implicit in any epistemology, and this fact creates acute problems when the subject under examination is human existence.

It is impossible to separate individual values from even the conception of an experiment or from any conclusion about whole human beings. Why is this? What is the relationship between values and epistemology?

Explanations about human beings fall into very few epistemological categories. Although it is possible to list several (Piaget lists six) epistemologies, I believe that their subdivision into subjective and objective categories has considerable heuristic value for reasons enumerated throughout this book. Over the years there has been a pendulum swing between the subjective, inward-turning epistemological stance and the objective, sense data, outward-turning focus.

The epistemological movement between subject and object indicates that neither position alone can fully grasp the way human beings come to know. The emphasis on either position as reflected in a given theory eventually reaches the limits of its possibility and critics then turn to the opposite stance with a new theoretical thrust. We have concluded that in order to explore fully a particular theoretical position, which may be either objective or subjective in focus, it is necessary to bracket the opposite epistemological tendency. The solution is not to attempt constant, leveled integrations of theories of psychological activity by attempting to equally balance subjective and objective tendencies, but rather to pursue one or the other approach while understanding that the bracketed possibility will need to be invoked at some time in the future when the frontiers of a theory have been reached. The pendulum swing of history between subjective and objective interpretations of human existence may very well indicate that a cyclical rather than a balanced approach to understanding human nature is what is indeed possible. Piaget's structuralism is the best example of neither yielding to a totally subjective nor objective point of view nor attempting to fuse the two. The cycle, however, has the quality of a spiral moving upward in that the theory describes increasing complexity in cognitive activity over the life span.

Every introductory psychology student has wondered why there are such different theories of human existence. Although there are not actually a great number of such theories, several appear to be different enough to give the impression of little coherence in the field. One answer, of course, is that psychologists know very little about human behavior and that all their attempts are fitful starts and stops that are doomed to failure. Perhaps as a result of our discussions so far, however, we can suggest another explanation, namely, that many psychological theories, most particularly those that have continued to influence thinking over the years, are all essentially correct even though on occasion they contradict one another. The contradictions generally stem from one of two theories overstepping its conceptual bounds by attempting to explain phenomena that it logically cannot explain.

We have seen examples of this in earlier chapters. For example, the attempt by behaviorists to explain language behavior and Gestalters to explain certain forms of learning were doomed to fail for this reason. The strength of any of these theories in comparison to any other, may be a function of the fact that it has been focused on an aspect of human behavior that exists at a conceptual level not intended by the other. Often, apparently contradictory theories represent *different ways of viewing human beings*. These different ways of viewing human beings can be quite diverse since a view of human existence is always permeated with the values and ethics of the viewer. This is also true when scientists discuss an amoeba, but the effect of experimenters' values on conclusions about that subject matter is minimal. Let it suffice to suggest, however, that it is possible to view an amoeba as either a medical entity or as the prototype for all human existence. Depending upon the point of view, one might get different emphases in an analysis of the structure and function of an amoeba. The example seems trivial and contradictions regarding a different view of amoebas are easily handled. However, a similar, more confusing competition among theoretical positions regarding man is more easily imagined. One might say that different psychological theories represent different images of man, as do different epistemological positions (subjective, objective).

Maurice Friedman has captured this point eloquently in his book *To Deny Our Nothingness: Contemporary Images of Man* (1967). Friedman suggested that different thinkers have seen human beings, for example, as political (Andre Mabraux, John Steinbeck, Ignazio Silone, Carlo Levi, Arthur Koestler), as vitalistic (Bergson, Kazantzakis), or as biological and psychological (Freud). Depending upon the perception one has of oneself and others, one will seek theory regarding human beings that is consistent with that conception. Certainly we can say that human beings are political, psychological, and vitalistic. The preference for which image of man is correct may be a matter of momentary or of long-term taste, a suggestion made, for one, by Merle Turner (1967).

VALUES

This is an age in which people are concerned with ethical and value issues in science, particularly those issues of a social nature. The public and federal and local governments have been concerned with experimentation on human beings performed by legitimate psychologists. We will need to examine this concern and then discuss values and their effect on psychological theory.

THE ETHICS OF PSYCHOLOGICAL EXPERIMENTATION

One of the manifestations of the last decade has been a decreasing amount of privacy in a quickly changing society coupled with an increasing concern about its loss. Besides the more usual concentration on government spying and the identification of citizens by easily retrievable numbers has been the concern with the presumed interference with the privacy of individuals by scientific enterprises. This concern is particularly directed toward medical, psychological, and sociological research.

The first criticism directed at scientists has concentrated upon two possible deleterious effects upon the public: that the privacy of an individual might be violated and that any questions regarding personal matters such as sex, marriage, or personality characteristics should not be intruded upon by the psychologist, sociologist, or medical experimenter. The second criticism is that an individual who is asked questions concerned with ordinarily very private types of activities may become eventually disturbed at the prospect of having to answer such questions. For example, asking someone about the nature of his sexual activities might very well bring about disturbances in the individual's psychological behavior if this happens to be a sensitive area. This second concern, of course, has been virtually the subject matter of clinical psychology for a long time and clinicians have developed ideas and techniques presumably to avoid the process of breakdown as a result of the discussion of certain sensitive topics between patient and therapist. To my knowledge, no one has objected to a clinical psychologist's attempt to gain information about an individual presumably for his own good, as long as he exercises caution.

Most objection has been directed at the issue of privacy. There is a concern that individuals are both used callously and that their privacy is violated by researchers who manipulate their subjects for their own (the researchers') purposes. The degree of outcry regarding violation of privacy is in direct proportion to the perceived privateness of the subject matter under investigation. Hence, an experimental psychologist investigating the individual's ability to discriminate brightness is rarely accused of violation of privacy. However, a clinical or social psychologist asking questions about the nature of the individual's sexual activities or political beliefs may very well be perceived as interfering with privacy. Most of the hue and cry has been directed against the researcher's dealing with human social problems. Thus the social psychologist receives most of the attack because of the nature of his interests. Social psychologists in America rarely attempt to solve a client's problems the way clinicians do. They are almost always pure researchers and they are consequently perceived to be detached from their subjects. This makes them maximally suspect because they do not even presume to help the subject, at least in the short run.

With these considerations and a growing political climate of egalitarian concerns, the American Psychological Association engaged in a virtual orgy of writing ethics for the conducting of experiments. Some of the initial efforts of this attempt resulted in a byzantine set of restrictions that would clearly have eliminated the possibility for all research into human affairs. The final product was a more reasonable attempt to alert the public and the researcher to the expectations of the American Psychological Association regarding reasonable and responsible behavior on the part of the experimenter toward the subject. These expectations can be interpreted to mean that if there seems to be any chance that the subject in an experiment can in any way be hurt by the process of the experiment, either physically or psychologically, the experimenter must desist. This, of course, is an ethic long shared by virtually all experimenters.

Clearly, there have been instances where experimenters did foolish things and actually did damage to an individual, both physically and psychologically. The instances were generally rare and the matter now is more a result of a national socio-political shift, obviously not unreasonable, toward more and more protection of the rights of individuals, even from presumably social-minded researchers. It is my opinion that, aside from responding to obvious cases of malpractice on the part of an experimenter, this concern with the ethics of experimentation is misplaced. The problem it seems to me, is minor and can be dealt with as abuses occur. A more major problem of values and ethics in psychology exists within the framework of theory type, that is, in interpretation of the nature of human beings. This is an extremely complicated issue, where there is, of course, no possibility of writing an ethics of procedure as there is in the case of laboratory or field experimentation. What is important, in my opinion, is to examine the latent value character of current theory types in psychology in order to understand what images of man are thereby projected.

VALUES IN SUBJECTIVE AND OBJECTIVE APPROACHES TO UNDERSTANDING HUMAN EXISTENCE

Joseph Wood Krutch wrote in 1929:

> The universe revealed by science, especially the sciences of biology and psychology, is one in which the human spirit cannot find a comfortable home. That spirit breathes freely only in a universe where what philosophers call Value Judgments are of supreme importance. It needs to believe, for instance, that right and wrong are real, that Love is more than a biological function, that the human mind is capable of reason rather than merely a rationalization, and that it has the power to will and to choose instead of being compelled merely to react in the fashion predetermined by its conditioning. Since science has proved that none of these beliefs is more than a delusion, mankind will be compelled to either surrender what we call its humanity by adjusting to the real world or to live some kind of tragic existence in a universe alien to the deepest needs of its nature [Krutch, 1956].

This was the thesis of Krutch's first edition of his book *The Modern Temper,* which was published in 1929. In 1956, when he revised the book, he no longer believed that science has proved that the value judgments of man and love as a humanizing force had been destroyed by scientific analysis. What is most interesting in this thesis is not so much that Krutch had come to reject the idea that science had made values illusory but what it proposes as possibilities for the fusion of science and values. This thesis also provides an accurate description of what adherence to certain epistemologies, mistaken or otherwise, can do to human values and what this, in turn, can do to the structure of society.

Krutch's observation contained in the quoted paragraph can be taken to represent a conclusion that is intrinsic to both the Freudian and general behaviorist positions. Both systems, as we have seen, are deterministic. Behavioral positions depend heavily on an analysis of external objects and their determining correlation with responses from the organism. The Freudian system, although not so heavily dependent upon the influence of external objects, disallows for the concept of free decision.

We have all too abundant information from convicted prisoners, survivors of concentration camps, and school children in autocratic schools, that it is possible to make an individual believe that he functions in a way determined by certain events and conditions that are immutable. It is not even necessary to use direct coercion to insure this belief. Let us assume that a child is brought up in the more or less usual manner for Americans, where he or she is on many occasions rewarded with candy, toys, and affection for doing things of which the parents approve and is punished with physical hurt and deprivation for doing things of which the parents do not approve. The patterns of reward and punishment follow a similar course during the child's formal education. He is then exposed to an interpretation of the nature of human existence where it is held that human beings are essentially passive and react to stimuli in the external environment in a manner that increases the likelihood of reward and decreases the likelihood of punishment.

There are innumerable specific instances of people apparently performing in this manner. We need only note that most people work very hard at performing long and sometimes complicated tasks principally in order to gain money, which then entitles them to a variety of more concrete rewards. It is not difficult for a world view to develop where most human activities are seen in terms of the maximization of reward and the minimization of pain. One also sees oneself as an object susceptible to rewards and punishments where these rewards and punishments may control most of life. This may not be a totally unreasonable view of human existence since it is clear that human beings *are* susceptible to rewards and punishments. It is equally clear, without enumerating the instances here, (we have done so throughout the book) that there are many situations that are not controlled by the administration of external or internal rewards unless "reward" is so general in its definition as to become meaningless, although some behaviorists do define reward in this manner. Most people live as if they have free choices available to them. They do not, day by day, perceive themselves as being the result of a series of determinations that can be traced actually or potentially. If they did, they would not insist on certain stances that they take with regard to politics, child raising, or God. However, it certainly is possible to perceive oneself as the passive recipient of either accidental or planned external influences out of one's control. In short, one can *become* a passive individual responding to external stimuli in the environment if one has the conception that there are no other alternatives for human existence.

If the "shaping" of behavior is emphasized by a social planner as the solution to various societal problems, and if people are convinced of this interpretation, it may become valid in a predictive sense because the application of shaping techniques can condition the individual without resistance on his part. He sees himself as having no choice in the matter, and therefore his view of the universe becomes, in part, what is forced upon him by the ideas of individuals around him. Because someone can be forced or coerced to respond to the process of shaping through reinforcement does not imply that the ordinary progress of his life is mostly or even partly influenced by this process.

Science changes the world it studies so that values are never separate from scientific enterprise and are colored by the particular theoretical or methodological approach to a given subject matter. There is always a methodology and a set of assumptions that any scientist brings to his study, although psychologists and others have not always believed that this was the case. Indeed, a total objectivity is not possible in the technical sense since conscious human response is never valueless. We have shown throughout this book that it is not logically possible to objectively examine many of the most important aspects of human existence. Values are one of those human endeavors not susceptible to objective analysis except for some of their peripheral characteristics.

I would suggest that an individual has a great deal of choice in the matter of perceiving himself as being determined by forces over which he has no control or seeing himself as being able to make free decisions regarding important matters. There is a sense in which we as individuals may freely permit ourselves to be used or examined as objects. That is, we may abdicate a great deal of our freedom to forms of control that result in our seeing ourselves and others as objects. There may very well be an economy of effort involved in such a tendency (all individuals engage in behaving and seeing themselves as objects from time to time). This economy of effort is perhaps also the best evolutionary explanation as to why individuals form attitudes.

An attitude is an emotionally laden tendency to react to a *class* of stimuli rather than to an individual of that class on his own terms. Whatever negative consequences this may have in a social sense, it does provide a certain efficiency in dealing with the environment. For example, should a professor attending a freshman class for the first time assume that these students will have certain attitudes and knowledge concerning the subject matter at hand, he will in most instances be correct. He may make grave errors for 1 or 2% of the class, but the efficiency of holding such an attitude may be a help in his instruction. The same is true for an individual freely choosing to see himself as an object in order to gain a certain efficiency in dealing with the vicissitudes of everyday life. For example, when being examined by a medical doctor (although some people prefer a bedside manner), many of us prefer to be totally treated as an object in order to correct our malady. For the sake of sanity and efficiency, it is extremely difficult to have subjective, personal, warm relationships too many times in any one day.

The fact that an objective confrontation among individuals is in some sense simpler to handle than a situation where one is treated as a totally functioning human being probably influences a great many individuals to be more comfortable with objective explanations of human existence. These are more straightforward and more easily uncovered than various kinds of subjective possibilities. It is also possible that although at any time it is possible to assert our ability to make free choices, we may have "forgotten" how to do so, or have fallen into the lethargy of easy economy and least effort in our relationships. The Milgram (1963) studies on order-following indicated some of the unfortunate possibilities of this sort.

ETHICS IN CLINICAL PSYCHOLOGY

The twentieth century has been called, among other things, the Age of Freud. This characterization can be meaningful within the context of sensual repression and its uncapping. Among other things, Freudian theory includes the idea of childhood polymorphus perversity. This is a label for the fact that children are extremely sensual and fuse easily with their environment both conceptually and physically. For example, the child has difficulty in separating its own body from parts of its environment. Thus, its own hand and a stone can be placed in the mouth. It feels uncomfortable when it is separated from its mother. We also know that abstracted reflection on the condition of human existence is minimal. The Freudian theory of neuroses, as we have seen, includes the basic idea that neurotic difficulty develops because of conflict that will naturally occur in the development of the human organism. One way of interpreting the conflicts that eventually yield to neuroses is to note that advancing adulthood separates the child both physically and psychologically from his environment, makes him more directed in his actions and more categorical in his conceptions of himself, other people and objects. This categorization can produce a conflict because these objects and people are separated from self. For example, sexuality becomes more specific. There are responses that are taboo for the adult that were not for the child who simply behaved in any manner so long as it was pleasurable.

In the 1920s, 1930s, and 1940s the Freudian sensibility concerning repressed sexuality diffused throughout the intelligensia and many of the middle classes. In Western countries with advanced technologies, which are predominantly Protestant, repressed sexuality as a societal phenomenon was eventually uncapped. Where at one time the main body of societal opinion was opposed to liberal sex mores, the climate has recently changed. Repressions of any sort are seen as evil and neurosis producing. In this respect, the Western world has undergone changes that could be predicted from an acceptance (not necessarily the validity) of a Freudian interpretation of existence.

The implication is that the child is happy in its polymorphus perversity and the adult is unhappy in its abstraction and repression. For about the last 15 years there has been an uncapping of adult restraints and the encouragement of a kind of adult polymorphus perversity. Traditional inhibitions have been weakened and the opposite tendencies have been loosed. Many traditional inhibitory agents such as the clergy and the law have supported the individual in removing his restraints and giving vent to his desires. The most explicit pornography is now legal in the United States, abortion has been legalized, and contraceptive devices are freely distributed. The young of the past decade have moved, if not in significant numbers at least with significant publicity, to living in communes where they share the most basic routines of life and presumably become more sensual in their experiences.

Were the release of repressed sexuality the sole result of the socially digested Freudian thesis, most of us would applaud. However, what has happened is not only that repressed sexuality has been released but also that the uncapping of one motivational area has led to the attempt, and indeed the political sanction, to uncap other motivations and emotions as well. The most negative by-product of this change is the significant increase in violence in the society. Because repression of any sort now seems worse than any inhibitions, the courts themselves in emphasizing rehabilitation indirectly support the process. When one begins to systematically uncap the rather fundamental desires of people, that society must bear a great deal of chaos. Those who judge and punish are no longer held in esteem, indeed they are seen as an antiegalitarian force. Justices and professors, politicians and police (in a sense the judges of society) become the most suspect when the uncapping process has reached significant heights. The society no longer, as Neitzsche expressed it, "honors pain and suffering." Rehabilitation becomes everything. The question then becomes what to rehabilitate people to, since the fundamental values of a society are of necessity challenged concomitant with the uncapping process.

A phenomenological existential psychology is perhaps best suited to understand the societal results of a deterministic Freudian-type effect. Hopefully, the task of the clinician is not to drive the individual who seeks help to the opposite end of the position where he finds himself. One does not try to bottle up sexual energy nor to release those inhibitions that are useful for the individual and the society. A classical criticism of Freudian theory is that this is precisely what happens. The task is always to find possibilities in life where a reasonable number of cyclical ups and downs occur. Judgment and inhibition cannot be eliminated nor can the free expression of many motivations and desires. Each age and each theoretical position seems to imply just that, that the extreme of the position advocated needs to be eliminated or severely controlled. Once again we find ourselves intertwined with issues of freedom, determinism, and responsibility. If one accepts responsibility he necessarily caps some of his own desires. If he gives free reign to various desires, he acts irresponsibly in some instances and can become dangerous to other people. The problem has always been to fuse freedom and responsibility to produce a viable synthesis analogous to the fusing in theory of ideas of subject and object. We have indicated above that such integrative fusion is probably not possible but that cycles of emphasis are. In therapy, I would suggest that cycles of similar possibilities involving an individual's emotional life constitute the best solution to many problems brought to the therapist.

Clearly, there is more than one way to view human existence. I suggest that one's view is extremely important for what type of therapy will be successful. There are more different approaches to therapy than there are theories of human behavior. All seem to be able to claim success with some of their patients. This is probably because commitment is an important underlying element to successful therapy. If a patient is committed to the form of therapy and the therapist practicing it, he is probably already on the road to being helped.

The question then becomes how does an individual become committed initially to therapy. Many therapists have recognized that their own personalities have been the attractive factor to their patients. They themselves as individuals, regardless of the therapy they practice or the theories they believe, have initially gotten an individual committed to whatever they want to do. If then an individual willfully enters, for example, behavior modification or Freudian therapy, there is a good chance he will benefit from it. The important reality for the patient is quite often the process of commitment and it is the making of this commitment for the therapist that becomes the critical pre-therapeutic event. We have already suggested that even in behavior modification therapy, which is an attempt to objectively remove problems for the individual, there is clearly an existential choice on the part of the patient to commit himself to this form of therapy. He must believe in its potential. And the belief in this potential is *outside of the frame of reference* of behavior modification or any other theory as an interpretation of human behavior. Commitment always involves values even if the commitment is to a scientific approach to the solutions of problems.

THE POLITICIZATION OF PSYCHOLOGY

One of the value contexts into which psychology fits is its relation to socio-political life. For most of the history of psychology and, indeed, of science, scientists have eschewed direct attempts to influence the political scene. They have sought to keep science separate from political and social influence. This is becoming more difficult. Increasingly, people insist on relevance to particular social problems from science. The issue of relevance is further complicated by the frequent suggestion that science in general and psychology in particular have served the needs of the establishment against the best interests of the people. Political interest in the results of the scientific enterprise is not new. In Russia, particularly during the 1930s with the work of Lysenko and others, there has been a consistent attempt to encourage research that yields results consistent with the establishment's political interpretation of life. (Lysenko had presumably discovered that certain acquired characteristics of wheat were genetically transmittable. This result was counter to all previous research to that time and later was demonstrated to be a politically motivated conclusion. It was consistent with the Russian socialist political belief that inherited rights were counter to a productive state.)

Recent accusations have been made that psychology has either been devoid of anything relevant to the people in general or has acted as a tool of the establishment. This attack, of course, is most frequently leveled at either clinical psychology or social psychology. Most recently a group of English social scientists have written a book called *Reconstructing Social Psychology* (Armistead, 1974). The editor, Nigel Armistead, suggested that the study of psychology and social psychology has nothing to do with life as it is lived or with issues of the world that consume it. Another criticism he made was that psychology and social psychology provide, through their theories, support for existing status quo political systems, whether they be in the Western world and therefore capitalistic in origin, or in the Eastern world and therefore Marxist in origin.

Armistead concluded that neither psychology nor sociology have the answers to the problems of relevance that he sought. To his credit, he also found that political revolutionaries with whom he was familiar in 1971 suffered from the same kinds of apparent lack of concern with relevance as did the psychologists and sociologists. They were more concerned with their own socio-political theories and the courses of actions that these dictated than with the problems and experiences of real people.

I would suggest that there is some confusion in Armistead's position, particularly concerning psychological work. As we have seen, a great deal of theory construction in psychology depends upon an objective experimental approach to its problems. We have seen that this kind of information can be of value over the long run and can act as a heuristic device for further hypotheses about the nature of human beings. However, it rarely satisfies questions of immediate relevance to either the individual or society. A phenomenological or experiential point of view is more likely to do this. One must examine, as we have done throughout this book, possibilities for both an objective, reductionistic type of approach to psychological and sociological issues, as well as the phenomenological approach in order to separate the possibilities for immediate relevance to social or other problems. It is, of course, true that certain individual and social problems cannot necessarily be solved at this or at any other time. Armistead apparently understood the differences between objective reductionistic approaches and phenomenological ones, but did not take this to be a clue to understanding why certain approaches to psychology cannot provide immediate social relevance. He therefore dismissed as irrelevant and unproductive the ''scientific'' approaches to human and social problems. In short, it is impossible to solve a current existential social problem with techniques (objective variety) that negate or are irrelevant to its very definition.

An even more telling criticism of Armistead's point is that it is extremely difficult to distinguish the relevancy of scientific research to immediate personal and social problems. A technique or theory that appears irrelevant to an individual personal or social problem at one point may not appear so a few months or a few years later. There is a case in point regarding some of my own research that has this quality.

Several years ago I was engaged in doing research on one of those reduced, attitudinal, social psychological problems that Armistead sees as dry and irrelevant regarding the order of persuasive communications and their effectiveness in changing opinions of a captive group in a laboratory setting. Various conclusions were drawn, the research was published, it was absorbed into the literature, and I forgot about it.

Several years later I had occasion to receive a call from two lawyers practicing in the state of Connecticut. They had just lost a case where their client had been charged with manslaughter. They believed the arguments in the case between the prosecution and the defense to be close and consequently assumed that the final arguments would be crucial to the decision of the jury. In the state of Connecticut, as well as in the vast majority of other states, the prosecution has the right to both open and close the final argument. Prosecution and defense receive equal amounts of time, but the prosecution may divide its time into an opening and closing statement. The lawyers believed this to be unfair and that it would unjustly bias the jury against their own defense presentation. They asked me if there was any social psychological research that would indicate that the final presentation and the arrangement of arguments could, ipso facto, influence the opinion of a group of listeners. It was clear from the research available that such was the case. There was equivocal data as to whether the first or second of the arguments presented to an audience would most influence them. However, there seemed to be little question that if an individual had the opportunity to present both the first and the last argument to a group who had not heard either pro or con arguments before, then that individual had a tremendous advantage. I wrote a letter to that effect citing literature and it was accepted as an exhibit in the case. The case, to my knowledge, is still in litigation. The point is, that here is an application of this dry, laboratory-oriented, objective research to a very real-life situation. I had no idea that it might be relevant to courtroom procedures when I did these studies, and indeed no one else suspected this either.

Since that time on two or three occasions lawyers have cited this literature with regard to increasing interest in the judicial procedure of the United States —a highly relevant social problem. Hence, the issue is not only whether psychology and sociology should or should not be of relevance to everyday life, but also that it is extremely difficult to determine whether it is or is not relevant at the time the research or the theory are developed.

Peter Sedgewick's (1974) article on ideology in modern psychology in the Armistead book made an interesting argument. The principal thesis is that the socio-cultural climate in which a psychologist finds himself distinctly influences the kind of theory he develops to explain human behavior. I believe the point is valid. One of Sedgewick's specific analyses is that the classical stimulus–response, drive reduction behaviorism conforms to the cold war "end of ideology" of the 1940s, 1950s, and 1960s, particularly in America. It is certainly true that modern behaviorism (after Hull) encouraged little theoretical analysis of concepts. This is mainly, as we have seen, a methodology where questions of who to change to what are outside of the framework of its tenets. There is a methodology to be put to anyone's use whatever his values. Certainly this is a nonideological position and I agree with Sedgewick.

Sedgewick's supplemental hypothesis is that a cognitive approach to theory about human beings would involve ideological theorists who would be principally concerned with an interpretation of reality rather than with methods to change an individual consistent with a yet-to-be-specified ideology. He sees this as an opening to the left in psychological theory. But it is clear that behaviorism can be used in the service of Marxism as well as in the service of capitalism. As a matter of fact, Russian psychology has tended to be physiological and behavioristic (and their politics are certainly to the left). I agree that behaviorism has a tendency to leave people in a situation in which they do not think about the nature of their own existence or the values that are part of that existence. Cognitive psychology might very well open up the possibility for such an examination. However, whether these positions have a right or left political coloration seems indeterminable and irrelevant. I can easily imagine a leftist-dominated regime utilizing behaviorism and its manifestations to their fullest. Sedgewick also pointed out that a cognitive paradigm of action, when allied with liberal politics, could motivate psychologists to engage in welfare activities such as the training of the disabled or the reduction of fatigue in monotonous tasks. However, these are precisely the types of tasks to which behavioral methods have been applied.

There is no doubt that psychological theories are quite often colored by the social–cultural contexts in which they find themselves. This is related to the point made above that apparently contradictory theories can be true at the same time. Certain manifestations of behavioral theory can produce effective ways of dealing with people's behavior if that behavior exists within a "nonideological" context (one wishes to lose his fear of snakes). A phenomenological theory is relevant to an individual who finds himself within a context where value and meaning are central. But to specify a left and right in psychological theory with regard to political position seems a fruitless task.

In the past it is certainly true that political entities of the right or left have identified themselves with various theories, but the ground for this has been largely gratituous and opportunistic rather than theoretical and well thought out. I would agree with Sedgewick (1974) and Gross (1974) that positivisms of all sorts have a tendency to depoliticize social science. It seems to me that this has both a good and a bad effect. The bad effect is that values are eschewed; the good is that one ends principally with method, and method can be used by individuals with any political suasion. If the technocracy that results from an emphasis on this form of behaviorism has a tendency to force directly or indirectly a nonthoughtful, nonideological, nonvalue-oriented view of life then indeed this should be corrected.

As a final point I would agree with Peter Sedgewick that the examination of Black IQ in comparison with White IQ or English IQ in comparison with Irish IQ is indeed a politically tinged cultural bias. The very choice of those couplings rather than any number of other possible ones (for example, rural–urban, German–American–Scandinavian infuses the problem with as many socio-political questions as scientific ones. Sedgewick's suggestion that the problem should first be examined from a cultural point of view and later from a scientific one is well taken.

References

Allport, G. The historical background of modern social psychology. In G. Lindzey & E. Aronson (Eds.). *The handbook of social psychology.* Reading, Massachusetts: Addison-Wesley, 1968.

Armistead, N. (Ed.). *Reconstructing social psychology.* Baltimore, Md.: Penguin, 1974.

Bandura, A. *Principles of behavior modification.* New York: Holt, Rinehart, & Winston, 1969.

Becker, H., & Barnes, H. E. *Social thought from lore to science.* Washington, D.C.: Harren Press, 1952.

Berger, P. L., & Luckmann, T. *The social construction of reality.* Garden City, N.Y.: Anchor, 1966.

Berne, E. *Transactional analysis in psychotherapy.* New York: Grove Press, 1961.

Boring, E. G. *A history of experimental psychology.* New York: Appleton Century Crofts, 1950.

Cattell, R. B. *The scientific analysis of personality.* Baltimore, Md.: Penguin, 1965.

Chomsky, N. *Current issues in linguistic theory.* The Hague: Moutin, 1964.

Chomsky, N. *Cartesian linguistics: a chapter in the history of rationalist thought.* New York: Harper & Row, 1966.

Darwin, C. *The origin of species.* London: Murray, 1859.

Descartes, Spinoza, Leibniz: The rationalists. Garden City, New York: Doubleday-Dolphin, (no date).

Deutsch, J. A. *The structural basis of behavior.* Chicago: University of Chicago Press, 1960.

Deutsch, J. A. The physiological basis of memory. *Annual Review of Psychology,* 1969, **20,** 85–104.

Deutsch, M., & Krauss, R. M. *Theories in social psychology.* New York: Basic Books, 1965.

Dollard, J., & Miller, N. E. *Personality and psychotherapy.* New York: McGraw-Hill, 1950.

Festinger, L. *A theory of cognitive dissonance.* Evanston, Illinois: Row Peterson, 1957.

Foa, U. G., & Foa, E. B. *Societal structures of the mind.* Springfield, Illinois: Charles C. Thomas, 1974.

Freud, S. *Beyond the pleasure principle.* New York: Bantam, 1959.

Freud, S. *The ego and the id.* New York: Norton, 1960a.

Freud, S. *Group psychology and the analysis of the ego.* New York: Bantam, 1960b.

Friedman, M. *To deny our nothingness: Contemporary images of man.* New York: Delta, 1967.

Goffman, E. *The presentation of self in everyday life.* Garden City, New York: Doubleday-Anchor, 1959.

Gross, G. Unnatural selection. In Armistead, N. (Ed.), *Reconstructing social psychology.* Baltimore, Maryland: Penguin, 1974.

Hebb, D. O. *The organization of behavior.* New York: Wiley, 1949.

Hubel, D. H., & Wiesel, T. N. Receptive fields of cells in striate cortex of very young, visually inexperienced kittens. *Journal of Neurophysiology,* 1963, **26,** 994–1002.

Hull, C. L. Mind, mechanism and behavior. *Psychological Review,* 1937, **44,** 1–32.

Hume, D. *A treatise of human nature.* Garden City, New York: Doubleday-Dolphin, 1961.

Husserl, E. *Cartesian meditation; an introduction to phenomenology.* The Hague: Nijhoff, 1960.

Husserl, E. *The idea of phenomenology.* The Hague: Nijhoff, 1964.

James, W. *Psychology (briefer course).* New York: Collier Books, 1962.

Janov, A. *The primal scream: primal therapy; cure for neurosis.* New York: Putnam, 1970.

Jones, E. *The life and work of Sigmund Freud.* New York: Basic Books, 1957.

Jung, C. G. *Two essays on analytical psychology.* Cleveland: Meridian, 1956.

Kant, I. *Critique of pure reason.* Garden City, New York: Doubleday-Dolphin, 1961.

Kelly, G. E. *The psychology of personal constructs.* New York: Norton, 1955.

Koch, S. Behavior as "intrinsically" regulated: work notes towards a pre-theory of phenomena called "motivational." In Marshall R. Jones (Ed.), *Nebraska Symposium on Motivation.* **Vol. IV.** Lincoln: University of Nebraska Press, 1956.

Koffka, K. *Principles of gestalt psychology.* New York: Harcourt, Brace, 1935.

Konorski, J. *Integrative activity of the brain.* Chicago: University of Chicago Press, 1967.

Krutch, J. W. *The modern temper.* New York: Harvest, 1956.

Lana, R. E. *Assumptions of social psychology.* New York: Appleton-Century-Crofts, 1969. (a)

Lana, R. E. Pretest sensitization. In R. Rosenthal & R. L. Rosnow (Eds.), *Artifact in behavioral research.* New York: Academic Press, 1969. (b).

Lana, R. E., & Rosnow, R. L. *Introduction to contemporary psychology.* New York: Holt, Rinehart, & Winston, 1972.

Lashley, K. S. The behavioristic interpretation of consciousness II. *Psychological Review,* 1923, **30,** 329–353.

Lévi-Strauss, C. *Structural anthropology.* New York: Basic Books, 1963.

Locke, J. *Essay concerning human understanding.* London: Basset, 1690.

Lorenz, K. *On aggression.* New York: Harcourt, Brace, & World, 1966.

Mach, E. *The analysis of sensation.* New York: Dover, 1959.

Machiavelli, N. *The prince.* New York: Mentor, 1952.

Marx, K. *Capital.* New York: Modern Library, 1936.

Maslow, A. *Toward a psychology of being.* Princeton, New Jersey: Van Nostrand, 1962.

McGuire, R. J., & Vallance, M. Aversion therapy by electric shock: a simple technique. *British Medical Journal,* 1964, **1,** 151–153.

Mead, G. H. *Mind, self, and society.* Chicago: University of Chicago Press, 1934.

Merleau-Ponty, M. *Phenomenology of perception.* New York: Humanities Press, 1962.

Merleau-Ponty, M. *The structure of behavior.* Boston: Beacon, 1963.

Merton, R. K. *Social theory and social structure* (rev. ed.). Glencoe, Illinois: Free Press, 1957.

Milgram, S. Behavioral study of obedience. *Journal of Abnormal & Social Psychology,* 1963, **67,** 371–378.

Monod, J. *Chance and necessity.* New York: Knopf, 1971.

Murphy, G., & Kovach, J. K. *Historical Introduction to Modern Psychology* (3rd ed.). New York: Harcourt, Brace, Jovanovich, 1972.

Nagel, E., & Newman, J. R. *Gödel's proof.* New York: New York University Press, 1958.

Nietzsche, F. *The genealogy of morals.* Garden City, New York: Doubleday-Anchor, 1956. (a)

Nietzsche, F. *The birth of tragedy.* Garden City, New York: Doubleday-Anchor, 1956. (b)

Nietzsche, F. *Beyond good and evil.* New York: Vintage, 1966.

Piaget, J. *Psychology and epistemology.* New York: Viking-Compass, 1971. (a)

Piaget, J. *Structuralism.* New York: Harper, 1971. (b)

Piaget, J. *Insights and illusions of philosophy.* New York: World, 1972.

Polin, R. *Nietzschean violence.* Paper given at Conference on Aggression and Violence in The History of Ideas, Third International Conference of the International Society for the History of Ideas, Philadelphia, Pennsylvania, 1972.

Pribram, K. H., A review of theory in physiological psychology. *Annual Review of Psychology,* 1960, **11,** 1–40.

Rank, O. *The trauma of birth.* New York: Harcourt, Brace, 1929.

Rogers, C. *Counseling and psychotherapy.* Boston: Houghton-Mifflin, 1942.

Rosenthal, R., & Rosnow, R. L. *Artifact in behavioral research.* New York: Academic Press, 1969.

Rotter, J. *Social learning and clinical psychology.* Englewood Cliffs, New Jersey: Prentice-Hall, 1954.

Russell, B. *A history of western philosophy.* New York: Simon & Schuster, 1945.

Rychlak, J. F. *A philosophy of science for personality theory.* New York: Houghton-Mifflin, 1968.

Sedgewick, P. Ideology in modern psychology. In N. Armistead (Ed.), *Reconstructing social psychology.* Baltimore, Maryland: Penguin, 1974.

Seigel, J. E. Violence and order in Machiavelli. Paper presented at the Conference on Aggression and Violence in The History of Ideas, Third International Conference of the International Society for the History of Ideas, Philadelphia, Pennsylvania, 1972.

Shaw, M. E., & Costanzo, P. R. *Theories of social psychology.* New York: McGraw-Hill, 1970.

Skinner, B. F. *Science and human behavior.* New York: Macmillan, 1953.

Skinner, B. F. *Verbal behavior.* New York: Appleton-Century-Crofts, 1957.

Sullivan, H. S. *The interpersonal theory of psychiatry.* New York: Norton, 1953.

Tolman, E. C. A behaviorist's definition of consciousness. *Psychological Review,* 1927, **34,** 433–439.

Toynbee, A. *A study of history.* New York: Oxford University Press, 1962.

Turner, M. B. *Philosophy and the science of behavior.* New York: Appleton-Century-Crofts, 1967.

Vico, G. *The new science of Giambattista Vico.* Garden City, New York: Doubleday-Anchor, 1961.

Watson, J. B. Psychology as the behaviorist views it. *Psychological Review,* 1913, **20,** 158–177.

Wolpe, J. *Psychotherapy by reciprocal inhibition.* Stanford, California: Stanford University Press, 1958.

Author Index

Numbers in *italics* refer to the pages on which the references are listed.

Subject Index

174